16.50

T

T

D0278596

Multi-microprocessor Systems

This is volume 18 in A.P.I.C. Studies in Data Processing
General Editor: Fraser Duncan
A complete list of titles in this series appears at the end of this volume

Multi-microprocessor Systems

Y. Paker

The Polytechnic of Central London, UK

1983

Academic Press

A Subsidiary of Harcourt Brace Jovanovich, Publishers
LONDON · NEW YORK
PARIS · SAN DIEGO · SAN FRANCISCO · SÃO PAULO
SYDNEY · TOKYO · TORONTO

ACADEMIC PRESS INC. (LONDON) LTD., 24/28 Oval Road, London NW1 7DX

United States Edition published by ACADEMIC PRESS INC., 111 Fifth Avenue, New York, New York 10003

British Library Cataloguing in Publication Data
Paker, Y.
   Multi-microprocessor systems.—(Automatic ·
Programming Information Centre studies in data
processing ISSN 066-4103;18)
   1. Microprocessors
   I. Title   II. Series
   001.64′04   QA76.5

ISBN 0-12-543980-6

LCCCN 82-72980

Typeset by CK Typesetters Ltd., 26 Mulgrave Road, Sutton, Surrey
Printed in Great Britain by St. Edmundsbury Press, Bury St. Edmunds, Suffolk

Preface

The quest for higher speed, higher performance and more reliable computers at lower costs (sometimes at any cost) goes on relentlessly. This is increasingly so today as the technologically advanced societies rely more and more on computers in nearly all aspects of life: central and local government, industry, commerce, defence and even leisure. Computers are not only replacing some traditional activities such as manual work on an assembly line, but are also giving rise to a whole new range of products and industries.

Even though current computing systems have progressed in a relatively short period of time over the last thirty years, in terms of tasks that they perform of data storage, retrieval, manipulation and input–output, their software and hardware concepts have not advanced very far from the early models. The next generation of computers are expected to handle far more complex systems, go beyond handling numbers and become capable of processing voice and pictures, run fully automated factories, fly inherently unstable aircraft, manage automated offices and so on , and communicate with humans interactively through speech and images. It is recognized that the next generation of computing systems, the so-called intelligent, knowledge-based systems, while taking advantage of the full power of circuit technology, will require new approaches to systems architecture.

Over the last decade, microprocessors have become key components feeding the progress of information technology. Extending the lower end of the computer spectrum, they have reduced computers to circuit components, thus opening up vast application areas. Their low cost has made computers available to practically everyone. Microprocessors also have helped the process of the convergence of computer and telecommunications technologies. Computers are no longer isolated point resources; their interconnection within a local or global framework is providing a whole new dimension, which is giving rise to structures better adapted to application requirements.

Microprocessors and ancillary circuits offer the designer a wide range of options, from a simple single-chip microcomputer up to a level of power and sophistication approaching conventional mainframe computers. The strides in the underlying circuit technologies continue and the rate of progress has yet to show signs of slowing down. The computing experience acquired over the last three decades, which has been the basis of the design of modern microprocessors, has made them very versatile components used for building a vast variety of systems as well as computers.

Microprocessors as powerful, and low-cost circuit components with relatively small size and power consumption, have brought a new design option whereby the aggregation of such devices can be used for a given application. Such structures are called multi-microprocessor systems.

There can be a variety of different motivations for building multi-microprocessor systems such as convenience, improved performance, high reliability and so on. For example, let us consider the performance factor. Fundamentally, progress in circuit technology could provide higher performance by faster clock rates (speed) and wider data paths (gate density). At a given stage of technological attainment, to improve performance, ingenuity could be applied to better arrange the given number of logic gates on a chip and/or a number of the same type of chips could be interconnected in some fashion to operate in parallel. The latter option assumes that an application could be defined as a combination of parallel processes. To improve reliability, the idea of using spare stand-by processors is an appealing possibility which favours a multi-microprocessor approach. Thus using a multiplicity of the same type, or a mix of microprocessors suitably interconnected is an important design option. This will become more important as we approach the technological limitations of circuit integration, hence the limited capabilities of a single microprocessor.

At the outset, although building multi-microprocessor structures appears attractive, in practice one encounters some problems. The fundamental difficulty comes from the fact that the principle of microcomputers, like all stored program computers, is sequential operation. In other words, their working is based on the execution of one operation at a time. This means that, whatever the complexity, an application needs to be formulated as a list of sequential instructions which is then handled by an operating system which itself consists of the same type of instructions. The execution of these atomic steps one after the other at a very high speed gives the impression of apparent simultaneity of various activities. On the other hand, when a number of microprocessors operate at the same time to handle a given application, this introduces parallelism into the basic architecture, not a straightforward proposition in a sequential environment. By contrast, analogue computers, being inherently parallel machines, adapt relatively easily to the functional requirements of an application.

Multi-microprocessors represent an important opportunity for novel architectural approaches in building computing systems to better suit given application requirements initially and also to adapt to changes during the system's life cycle. The semiconductor manufacturers have recognized this. The newer types of microprocessors have features which enable them to be interconnected via a common shared bus. Recent work in local area networks is providing a framework to connect a number of micro-processors. Yet there is no coherent approach in building such systems to take advantage of modularity. Multi-microprocessor systems can still be considered in the experimental research phase.

This text is written to describe the main issues involved in the building of multi-microprocessor systems. This is done by taking into account the current state of the art and likely future developments. The commercially available microprocessor is taken as the basic building block. It is recognized that very large scale integration (VLSI) provides many opportunities for introducing parallelism within a chip. Unfortunately, this option is only available to a few organizations with access to VLSI design and production facilities. In the text, the subject is treated at the level of systems architecture, without entering too much into detailed circuit design aspects. The major architectural approaches, interconnection schemes and related software issues are considered at some length. To illustrate the concepts introduced, numerous machines are referred to as examples. Care is taken, however, to ensure a balanced presentation so that one particular example does not overshadow the whole text. One architectural approach, the variable topology multicomputer, developed by myself and my colleagues, is perhaps given slightly more coverage than the others.

In the text a new set of symbols are proposed to identify various basic components of a multi-microprocessor system such as an individual processor, memory, bus, etc. A full complement of these symbols can be seen in Fig. 1.9. It is hoped that this new representation will, at a glance, enable the reader to extract the major architectural features as well as identify the functions of each block, without the necessity of explicitly writing this on the diagram. Note that the symbols chosen are either those used for flow-charting or a combination of these shapes. The intention is that a standard flow-charting template, which can be obtained easily, can be used to draw these diagrams. It is expected that this convention will help the reader to understand better the diagrammatical representation of various architectures presented. Furthermore, I hope that this representation will have a much wider acceptance and be adopted by microprocessor designers.

The text commences with an overview of current microprocessors, their classification and a comparative presentation of the main architectural features of a number of well-known types. In Chapter 2 a historical background to the development of multi-microprocessors is presented with examples. Then a classification for multi-microprocessor structures is given. In Chapter 3 the main motivations for building multi-microprocessor systems and various possible architectural approaches are discussed in depth. Chapter 4 then deals with interconnection and communication aspects. Thus a common bus such as MULTIBUS, a contention bus such as Ethernet, a loop such as the Cambridge ring and network structures such as the variable topology multicomputer are treated in some detail. Chapter 5 considers the point of view of a systems designer and the main issues and options available for building a multi-microprocessor system. Chapter 6 covers the important problem of software for which there are a number of different approaches, yet few generally accepted rules. The software problem is covered by discussions of the operating system, communication and language aspects. A number of examples such as MICROS, CHORUS, MEDUSA and others are mentioned. Finally, the problem of building highly reliable computers taking advantage of the redundancy that is inherent in a multi-microprocessor system constitutes Chapter 7. Included are hardware and software redundancy issues and reconfigurable systems that can sustain some failures, yet are able to continue operation with some loss of performance.

It is hoped that this book will serve researchers and students of computer architecture as well as managers and design engineers in industry to better understand the underlying principles, opportunities and difficulties in building multi-microprocessor systems. This is a very rapidly changing field, yet with every new generation of microprocessors the motivation for their use in large numbers is becoming even greater. To cope with the requirements of the next generation of computers, multi-microprocessors are bound to play an important part.

This book is the culmination of my 'work in real-time, parallel and distributed computing over a number of years, supported by the Science and Engineering Research Council, UK, United States European Research Office, the Polytechnic of Central London and Rennes University, France. I gratefully acknowledge the support that I have received. An international seminar in multi-microprocessor systems that I organized at PCL with INRIA in 1978, many courses and meetings, visits and discussions with various research groups in Europe and USA contributed much to this book. I am, therefore, grateful to the many people who directly or indirectly helped in the writing of this text. In particular I should like to mention the contribution of Dr M. Bozyigit who worked with me on the variable topology multi-computer project. Finally the high quality of drawings owe much to the meticulous work of Carol Hughes, of the Audio Visual Aids department of the Polytechnic of Central London.

February 1983 Y. Paker
London

To Ruth

Contents

Chapter 1

Introduction to Microprocessors

1.1 Overview of Microprocessor Technologies and Trends

The availability of low cost yet increasingly more powerful microprocessors and related high-density integrated circuits is opening up new application areas which were inconceivable only a few years ago. The rapid technological progress that we have been experiencing in microelectronics, which has been a major driving force in the computer industry, does not appear to be levelling off and is expected to continue at the same rate for some years to come, till the mid-eighties and possibly beyond [1]. The usual method of indicating this progress is to draw a graph showing the number of components (or transistors) that can be built on a single chip. The year 1959 is taken as the origin, where the first planar transistor was built. The simple straight line plot, the so-called Moore's law [2], is remarkable in that it shows that the number of components that can be placed on a chip doubles every year; a unique human experience in technological progress (Fig. 1.1).

It is customary to differentiate the various stages of development of integrated circuits as shown in Table 1.1. The figures given in this table should be considered as order of magnitude quantities. The implications of each stage, however, in digital electronics and computer design have been crucial. For example, small scale integration (SSI) provided elementary logic functions which previously had to be built using discrete components (transistors, resistors). Medium scale integration (MSI) then provided logical building blocks, each incorporating several logic functions. At each stage the reliability improved, and the cost and power consumption per function decreased. This made it possible to design and build more and more complex circuits using functional blocks.

This progression, however, could not follow the same pattern when transition had to take place to large scale integration (LSI). MSI technology

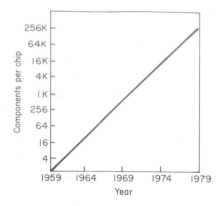

Year

Fig. 1.1   The number of components per chip as a function of time.

has been able to produce a consistent set of circuits (building blocks) to satisfy most requirements for manufacturing a computer or complex digital systems. In fact a number of technologies have been developed like TTL (transistor transistor logic), ECL (emitter coupled logic) and others to satisfy performance, speed, and other specific requirements.

Table 1.I   Progress in integrated circuits.

	Component per chip	Year
Small scale integration (SSI)	1–10	1960–65
Medium scale integration (MSI)	10–1000	1965–70
Large scale integration (LSI)	1000–100 000	1970–80
Very large scale integration (VLSI)	100 000–(1 000 000)	1980–

LSI, and later on very large scale integration (VLSI), on the other hand, made it possible to build a complete digital system on a single chip. To ensure the widest possible utilization of a given circuit type, which is the main objective of the semiconductor manufacturers geared for volume production, it had to be as versatile as possible. This principle demonstrates the success of microprocessors, where a single chip can be used for many different purposes by simply changing the program stored in its memory. Thus we observe that while the custom-specified circuits are technically feasible to manufacture, because of the high costs involved this is possible only for big consumers like the automobile and communication industries. The main trend, however, is to standardize and reduce the types in the VLSI industry, in particular microprocessors, memory, and auxiliary circuits. The vast market that exists for a few standard types of microprocessors is ensuring the increased volume of production, hence reduction of costs.

Thus a microprocessor has now become a standard VLSI circuit element for the design and construction of a majority of digital systems, opening up new and unexplored application areas.

Currently the most successful technology used for building a micro-processor is the MOS (metal oxide silicon) process, in which a silicon wafer is used as the basic substrate to build transistors, using photo-etching, doping, and metal evaporation techniques. A measure of power of a VLSI chip is the number of gates per chip multiplied by clock speed, per gate. The current figure for this is 10^{11} gate–hertz. A US Department of Defence Project is currently underway to achieve a figure of 10^{13} gate–hertz [3]. Advances in silicon fabrication techniques alone contributed to the achievement of the current figure by increasing chip area (better yield), by introducing innovative circuits, and by scaling down the dimensions of gates and interconnections. The above project has the objectives of producing, in 1986, a processor containing 250 000 gates, operating at clock speeds of at least 25 MHz and performing between several million and several billion operations per second. The ultimate limit of MOS technology is seen as a circuit (CMOS-Complementary MOS) that will operate with a supply voltage of 400 mV, a minimum line width of $0 \cdot 25$ μm, dissipate 1 W at an operating frequency of 100 MHz with a chip size of 50×50 mm^2 and complexity of 100 million gates [4]. Currently, a typical complex micro-processor available is the Motorola 68000 which contains 70 000 transistors and operates at 8 MHz.

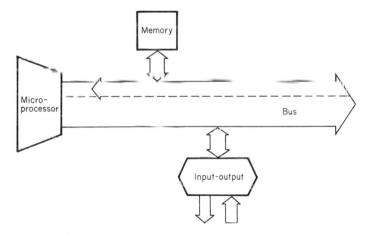

Fig. 1.2   Structure of a microcomputer.

At this stage it is perhaps necessary to give a definition of a micro-processor. It is a single integrated circuit containing all the functions of a central processing unit of a stored program digital computer. For a microprocessor to become an operational unit the minimum requirements are memory and some input–output devices. A microprocessor with memory and input–output units constitutes a digital computer which can be called a microcomputer, as shown in Fig. 1.2. Note the different shapes used for the functional components. If a single integrated circuit contains all the three elements (processor, memory, and input–output) then this is called a single-chip microcomputer. There is another approach, so-called bit-slice machines, where a central processor is built using a set of LSI circuits and memory. Normally these are microprogrammed processors where the user defines the microcode which is then stored in microprogram memory. In this case such a processor does not qualify as a microprocessor according to the above definition. Unlike a bit-slice processor, in a microprocessor there is no possibility of having access to the internal control signals nor of making changes, such as adding more instructions. The only means of interaction between a microprocessor and the outside world is the external bus.

1.2   Microprocessor Classification

To understand the various types of microprocessors that are available today it is worthwhile considering the historical progress that has taken place since 1971, when Intel introduced the 4004, a 4-bit machine intended for calculator applications [5]. This was designed essentially for serial binary coded decimal (BCD) operations. About the same time Intel was working on another 8-bit processor, the 8008, which was introduced in 1972. This had a simple architecture: byte handling facilities, a memory space limited to 16 kbytes and a small instruction set with a few operand addressing modes. The 8080 that was introduced in 1974 was still an 8-bit machine but with 64 kbyte memory space, increased instruction set, stack handling capability and more complete addressing modes, including limited handling of 16-bit words. In 1975 Zilog introduced the Z-80 microprocessor which was compatible with the 8080. Other semi-conductor companies produced similar microprocessors such as Motorola, National Semiconductor, Texas Instrument and others. In 1978 Intel produced the 16-bit microcomputer 8086, although Texas Instrument's 9900 preceded this as a 16-bit micro-processor. In 1979 Zilog introduced the Z8000 and in 1980 Motorola introduced the MC68000, both 16-bit microprocessors. It is known that semiconductor manufacturers are now working on 32-bit machines, some having already produced prototypes, which will possibly become widely available during the mid eighties.

We can differentiate essentially three types of microprocessors.

Single-chip Microcomputers

Single-chip microcomputers are complete microcomputers where processor, memory, and input–output, as well as auxiliary electronics such as clock oscillators, are all integrated on a single chip. They follow the tradition of the first 4-bit microprocessors. The silicon area that the advanced technology makes it available is used to integrate more functions such as memory, input–output, rather than increase the power and architectural complexity of the processor. Such a circuit computer contains, typically, a small data memory of 64–256 bytes and a program memory (ROM—read only memory) of about 2 kbytes. The program memory is fixed during the manufacturing process and therefore it needs to be defined during the masking stage. This is an expensive option available only for volume customers. Intel produces a relatively more expensive microcomputer model with EPROM memory for low volume users. The first such single-chip microcomputer was introduced by Intel in late 1976 (MCS-48) [6]. More recently Zilog produced a similar microcomputer, the Z-8, and Motorola the MC6081.

Single-chip microcomputers are meant for low cost, high volume embedded applications such as in home appliances, video games, cars, etc.

In a multi-processor environment, in spite of the low cost advantage (which is important when building machines with large numbers of such components), the restricted input–output facilities, memory size, and the computing power of single-chip microcomputer makes them unattractive for such applications. They are ideally suited to perform a well-defined function where requirements can be met with the limited processing power and memory available with such circuits. In this text such single-chip microcomputers will not be considered.

General Purpose Microprocessors

General purpose microprocessors are the 8-bit microprocessors with proven architecture which have attained today a certain level of maturity. They are low cost, yet have considerable computing power, intended for wide-ranging general purpose markets. Normally, a well-integrated family of circuits exist such as various memory types, serial and parallel input–output circuits, clock and DMA (direct memory access) circuits so that a designer has flexibility to assemble those circuits which are required by the specifications. Intel 8085, Zilog Z-80 and Motorola MC6800 are typical examples of such machines. Vast amounts of software have already accumulated for these machines.

High Performance Microprocessors

High performance microprocessors are 16-bit machines at the fore-front of technology where the aim is to achieve minicomputer performance. Moving from 8- to 16-bit processors represents a quantum jump for the manufacturers where some preferred to have a fresh start rather than be restricted in design options due to compatibility considerations. One common point about the 16-bit microprocessor is the ability to handle large memory space and the introduction of memory management techniques by an additional circuit (Fig. 1.3). For example, the Z8000 can directly access 8 Mbytes of address space and there are six such distinct address spaces allocated for distinct purposes such as instruction, data, stack, etc. In addition to more powerful instruction set and data manipulation capabilities, such microprocessors separate system and user modes, making it easier to implement multi-task applications. Clearly, the instruction set is also aimed at providing a suitable environment for high-level language implementation.

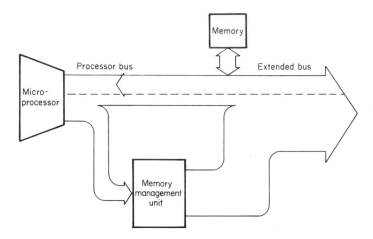

Fig. 1.3 High performance microprocessor.

Finally, these microprocessors include hardware features aimed at connecting a number of them in a multi-microprocessor configuration. This will be considered in more detail.

1.3   Microprocessor Architectures

Different forces have been at play in the design of the microprocessor, depending on the technological constraints, market demands, and the types of microprocessors, as explained above. For the single-chip microcomputer market the emphasis has been to incorporate more functions, hence a reduction of external circuits, in some cases even analogue functions, rather than improve computational power or increase memory. Hence the main objective has been to lower the overall hardware costs due to the use of a microcomputer, which results in the reduction of external electronics. In some applications this requirement may become crucial, say, due to weight or size limitations. The cost of software due to restricted memory, is not considered an important factor, more so since it is shared among many thousands to millions of units manufactured.

General purpose microprocessors have been designed to provide a decent processing capability, to satisfy a vast variety of applications, embedded or otherwise. Thus the silicon space available has been utilized to improve processor capabilities in terms of instruction set, addressing, and internal registers. In the mid seventies limited technology imposed the 8-bit word size, but experience with such microprocessors shows that they permitted the construction of amazingly wide-ranging embedded systems, as well as general purpose computers, albeit of restricted performance. Yet increasingly software has become an important factor, constituting from 50 to 90% of the cost of new designs [7].

It is not surprising, then, that high performance microprocessors are designed with a view to providing as many features as possible to support high-level languages and systems programs. In that sense they constitute a departure from the 8-bit architecture. The technological advances are exploited boldly to produce microprocessors compatible with the power and performance of current minicomputers, and to introduce new architectures more with a view of being compatible upward (by the addition of more facilities and perhaps compatibility with the future 32-bit machines) rather than maintaining compatibility with the current 8-bit machines. In the computer industry the introduction of a brand new machine line is costly. Thus the advent of the 16-bit machines indicates the confidence of the manufacturers in the future, and this belief that high-level languages will become a major software development tool for microcomputers.

For a systems designer, using a microprocessor presents certain opportunities since there is full access to the external bus of the processor. This is not true of a minicomputer, where access occurs via an input–output device. On the other hand, no internal processor signals are available to the systems designer. Therefore the understanding of the functioning of a microprocessor's external bus is essential. The external bus also provides a means of standardization where devices can be built to be interfaced to a given bus. Currently, each manufacturer maintains its own bus standard and provides compatible circuits. Memory, however, is a notable exception where de facto accepted standards exist, clearly to everyone's benefit.

In this section, without attempting to be comprehensive, brief outlines of general purpose and high performance microprocessors are given, concentrating on processor facilities from the point of view of the user. Internal logic organization and architecture is not discussed.

General Purpose Microprocessor Architecture

A microprocessor's architectural features can be considered under the following categories: (1) central processor unit (CPU) resources, (2) instruction set, (3) addressing, (4) processor bus and input–output handling.

CPU resources

CPU resources are internal registers and facilities that are wired in for handling various data formats, stacks, interrupts, context switching, and recording of various conditions (status word). It is useful to summarize some of the above features with respect to a specific microprocessor, namely the Zilog Z-80 [8], which is widely used and representative of the state of the art in this category (compatible also with Intel 8080).

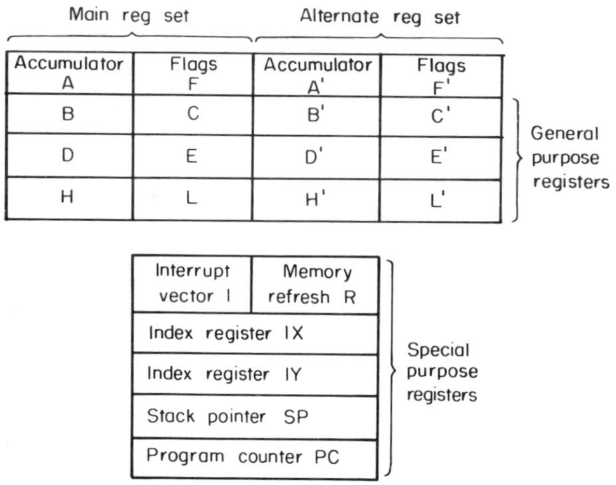

Main reg set		Alternate reg set		
Accumulator A	Flags F	Accumulator A'	Flags F'	
B	C	B'	C'	General purpose registers
D	E	D'	E'	
H	L	H'	L'	

Interrupt vector I	Memory refresh R	
Index register IX		Special purpose registers
Index register IY		
Stack pointer SP		
Program counter PC		

Fig. 1.4 Z-80 CPU register configuration.

In Fig. 1.4 the CPU registers of the Z-80 are shown. These consist of a group of 8-bit registers (general purpose) and a second group of 16-bit registers, special purpose registers dedicated for specific functions. In certain situations two 8-bit registers can be paired to form a 16-bit register. Only one 8-bit register (A) can be used for arithmetic/logic operations with associated 8-bit flag register (F) to record various conditions. Restricted

16-bit operations are possible mainly for address calculations. A hardware stack is implemented by means of the 16-bit stack pointer (SP) register. The 8-bit interrupt register supports external interrupt requests where the interrupting device provides an 8-bit lower address. This, when combined with the interrupt vector (I) register yields a 16-bit address for an indirect call to an interrupt routine: it is interesting to note that interrupt also uses the stack. The alternative register set shown in Fig. 1.4 can be used to swap with the main register set to provide fast context switching. This is a useful feature when several concurrent tasks are to be handled.

Instruction set

An instruction set design is the outcome of many factors, often conflicting. For general purpose microprocessors, the size of data handled being a byte, instructions exist to handle bytes and, in a more restricted manner, words (16-bit). One tries to make the instruction format compact, so as to achieve efficient use of memory. Thus, for example, the Z-80 has single and double byte operation codes. One also attempts to have an instruction set which is as complete as possible, i.e. a given instruction is applicable for all addressing modes and their combinations. The generality of an instruction set improves programming efficiency.

The Z-80 instruction repertoire includes instructions for the transfer of data between internal register-to-register, memory-to-internal register and memory-to-memory. Instructions exist for stack handling (PUSH, POP). There are instructions to transfer blocks of consecutive bytes in the memory and to search for a given byte in a block of bytes. Limited facilities for handling 16-bit data exist, in particular to help with address handling.

The arithmetic/logic capabilities of general purpose microprocessors are rather restricted. Normally byte arithmetic (2's complement form) is provided. In a more restricted fashion 16-bit arithmetic is made available in order to manipulate addresses.

Program flow control is achieved by JUMP (conditional or unconditional) and CALL instructions. The latter serves for subroutine construction where the processor stack facility is used automatically. Interrupt is also implemented as an external CALL instruction pointing to a subroutine where the indirect address is provided by the external device and internal register, as explained above.

Addressing

Memory space in this category of microprocessors is restricted to 64 kbytes specified by a 16-bit word address. The direct addressing is used within this address space (no segmentation). Normally data addressed is a byte, or a word if it refers to an address. For example, the Z-80 implements immediate addressing for byte and word, extended addressing where 16-bit operand address follows the instruction, and indexed addressing using the two index registers (X) and (Y) (Fig. 1.4). Register pairs can also be used for addressing memory in register indirect addressing mode. Operands can be in register (register addressing) or implied (such as for arithmetic operations), in which case a specific register (such as A) is used.

Processor bus and input-output handling

Processor bus is the medium for all memory and input–output connections. The external connections of the Z-80 processor are shown (Fig. 1.5) to illustrate the signals that are used to constitute the processor bus. It consists of a 16-bit address bus to cover the 64 kbyte memory space and an 8-bit bi-directional data bus for byte transfers to and from the processor. The system control indicates the direction of the flow of data (RD: read, WR: write). The memory and input–output space is separated by MREQ (memory request) and IORQ (input–output request) lines. The Z-80 uses only the lower 8-bit address bus for input–output addressing (256 devices total). The line RFSM provides the signal necessary for the refresh function of dynamic memories. Finally M1 indicates the fetch cycle of the processor. The microprocessor bus operates in an asynchronous fashion to enable the connection of devices of different speed. This is achieved by the WAIT input of CPU control lines. This is an important signal which causes the

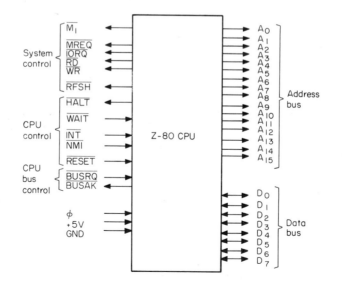

Fig. 1.5   Z-80 CPU signals.

CPU to enter a "wait" state as long as this signal is active. The other two lines INT and NMI refer to maskable and non-maskable interrupt inputs respectively. RESET is used to initialize the CPU.

CPU bus control lines serve to establish a master–slave relationship between two units on the same bus. Normally the CPU is the bus master. However, if an external device requests it via a BUSRQ active input, the processor, after completing its current machine cycle, relinquishes the bus by a BUSAK active. The device signals to the processor the completion of the transaction by BUSRQ inactive, when the processor resumes the role of bus master. This mechanism will be discussed in more detail in Chapter 4.

High Performance Microprocessors

As stated above, high performance 16-bit microprocessors attempt to achieve the performance of a minicomputer. Thus one observes many of the current aspects of minicomputer architecture in the high performance microprocessors. Yet some of the architectural features go beyond the minicomputer standards. This is so because the technology has reached a stage where chip complexity is no longer a major restrictive factor. Therefore the experience gained in computer architecture over the last twenty-five years can now be applied to the design of advanced micro- processors. The software bottleneck that became a considerable problem for the 8-bit machines also has received much attention. The consensus has been that the 16-bit microprocessors have to support high-level languages and features to implement an operating system. In comparison to the general purpose microprocessors, there are certain characteristics of 16-bit machines that stand out, such as vastly improved memory space, the ability to handle various types of data, improved instruction set including more powerful arithmetic capabilities, symmetry, and completeness in instruction set as far as addressing modes are concerned. Facilities exist for context switching, interrupt, and trap handling. Extensive stack handling is clearly intended for high-level language development. Segmentation is supported, sometimes by means of an additional integrated circuit(s). The circuit pin limitation creates a severe constraint. This has forced manufacturers either to go for a 64-pin circuit or to offer two versions: either 40-pin unsegmented or 64-pin segmented. Here we consider some of the architectural features in more detail. To illustrate, we consider three well-known microprocessors: the Intel 8086 (1978), Zilog Z8000 (1979), and Motorola MC68000 (1980).

CPU resources

The CPU resources, reflecting the advances in technology, have been dramatically improved in terms of size (16-bit), number, capability, flexibility, and general purpose use of processor registers. In Fig. 1.6 we show the internal registers of the 8086, Z8000, and MC68000.

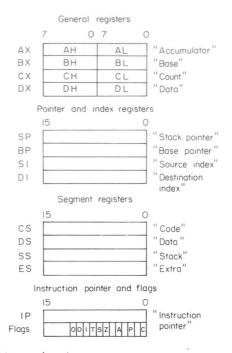

Fig. 1.6a   The 8086 internal register structure.

The Intel 8086 processor contains a total of thirteen 16-bit registers and nine 1-bit flags (Fig. 1.6a) [5]. These can be considered under three groups of four registers. The first set, general registers, allows byte and word handling, and is compatible with the 8080 register set. The second set consists of 16-bit registers, each being used for certain specific functions such as stack handling and indexing. Essentially this set is used for address manipulation. The third set is used for addressing where the 8086 differentiates address spaces for data, code, and stack.

In contrast, Z8000 architecture uses a general purpose register approach where there are 16 16-bit registers, as shown in Fig. 1.6b [9]. With very few exceptions these can be used interchangeably. The first eight registers allow handling bytes. Registers can be paired for 32-bit long word handling. In a few cases like multiply and divide, register quadruples are used to form 64-bit registers. All registers can be used for stack and indexing purposes [10].

The Motorola MC68000 architecture divides internal registers into two classes [11]. Eight 32-bit data registers which can be used for byte, word,

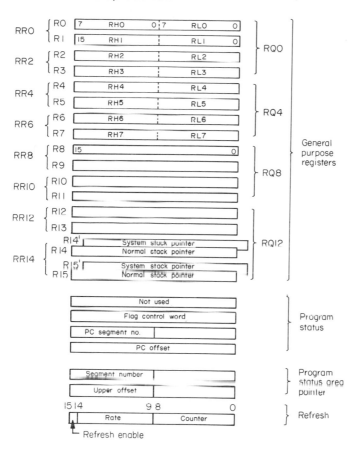

Fig. 1.6b The Z8000 internal register structure (segmented version).

and long word operations. In addressing they can serve as indexes. The remaining eight 32-bit registers serve for addressing purposes, one with the special function of stack pointer (Fig. 1.6c).

The interrupt mechanism of the 8086 is similar to the approach of the 8080. The interrupting device provides a byte that is used to index a table of subroutine addresses. The subroutines can reside anywhere in the memory. The Z8000 has three kinds of interrupts: non-maskable, non vectored, and vectored. In addition, five traps exist: system call, illegal instruction, privileged input–output instruction, other privileged instructions, and the segmentation trap. When interrupts or traps occur, the old program status is pushed onto the system stack with one more word that usually indicates the reason for the trap occurrence. A new program status is fetched from the new program status area which is indicated by the new program status area pointer (Fig. 1.6b).

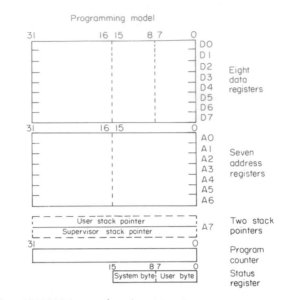

Fig. 1.6c   The MC68000 internal register structure.

The microprocessor MC68000 combines all the facilities of interrupts and traps under the name of exception processing. Thus a processor can be in normal (instruction execution), exception, and halt state. The exception state arises due to an external interrupt, internal trap instruction, tracing, and other unusual conditions such as bus error. The exception handling provides a mechanism of context switching where the old status register is copied, and the vector of the exception is determined to fetch the new processor status. The MC68000 also provides a user and supervisor state to ensure better security. Thus in the supervisor state certain privileged instructions can be executed. The operating system runs at supervisor state, having access to all system facilities. The change from user to privileged state is done through exception handling. The Z8000 microprocessor also differentiates the system and normal modes with different access rights to hardware facilities.

Instruction set

Instruction sets for 16-bit microprocessors are remarkably extensive and varied. While the 8086 has maintained compatibility with the 8080 by including the latter instruction set as a subset, both the Z8000 and the MC68000 have departed from the earlier models by introducing completely new instruction sets.

We deliberately avoid a detailed discussion of the instruction set for the three high-performance microprocessors considered. Here it is sufficient to state that extensive instructions exist for data transfers, mainly between processor registers and memory, arithmetic and logic instructions including 16-bit multiply/divide, program control and input–output instructions. In comparison to the 8-bit microprocessor, the instruction set of the 16-bit microprocessor is capable of handling a variety of data types like byte, word, double word, string, and includes a more extensive range of addressing modes which will be discussed later. The instruction set of these microprocessors also contains some specialized instructions to implement synchronization functions such as semaphores, and control for multi-processor applications.

Addressing

The outstanding difference with the 8-bit microprocessors is the extended memory space and the introduction of segmentation techniques. The memory addressing mechanism used for the 8086 and Z8000 are shown in Figs 1.7a and b. The MC68000 uses a 32-bit address format. The current implementation with 23 address lines allows direct addressing of 8 Mwords.

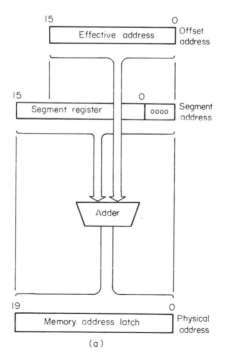

(a)

Fig. 1.7a   Memory management: logical to physical address translation in the 8086.

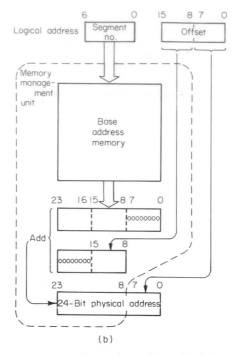

Fig. 1.7b   Memory management: logical to physical address translation in the
Z8000.

The 8086 memory space is 1 Mbyte (20-bit address). Physical addresses are
obtained by means of a segment register, the contents of which are added to
the 16-bit addresses used. The Z8000 requires an additional memory
management circuit to provide segmentation. The 24-bit physical address is
obtained by means of a segment number and offset value as shown in

Table 1.II   Addressing modes for MC68000.

1. Data register direct
2. Address register direct
3. Address register indirect
4. Address register indirect with post-increment
5. Address register indirect with pre-decrement
6. Address register indirect with displacement
7. Address register indirect with index
8. Absolute short address
9. Absolute long address
10. Program counter with displacement
11. Program counter with index
12. Immediate data

Fig. 1.7b. On the processor chip, signals exist to differentiate between the data, code, and stack, in both system and user modes. Therefore, a designer could separate memory allocated for different purposes. This mechanism allows also for expansion of the memory space by up to six times.

Extensive addressing modes exist for 16-bit microprocessors. For example, for the MC68000 the full addressing modes are listed in Table 1.II. Various addressing modes are also used to help to set up stacks and queues.

Processor bus and input–output handling

Processor bus is the medium used for connection to memory and other input–output devices. The pressures are thus to have a wide processor bus to handle 16-bit data and a large scale memory. The standard that a bus provides is very important since all external devices are connected through the bus, and hence need to be compatible with it.

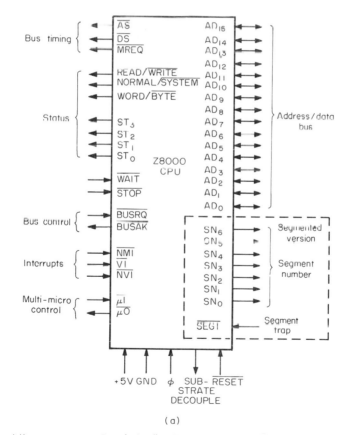

(a)

Fig. 1.8a   Microprocessor signals in the Z8000.

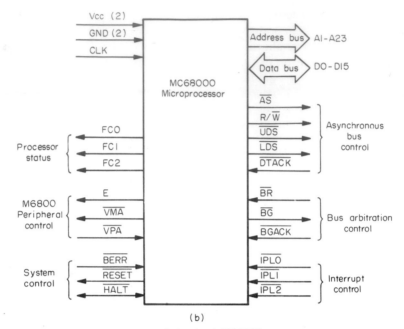

Fig. 1.8b   Microprocessor signals in the MC68000.

Processor bus also constitutes the external connections to a micro-processor where the pin restrictions severely limit its size. The manufacturers have adopted either a large circuit packaging with 64 pins like the Motorola MC68000 or a 48-pin package with an additional integrated circuit for memory management to achieve an extended size bus like the Z8000. To compare these two approaches the Z8000 and MC68000 buses are shown in Figs 1.8a and b respectively [9], [12].

Table 1.III   Processor status signals.

Z8000 (ST0-ST3)	MC68000 (FC0-FC2)
Memory request	User data
Stack pointer request	User program
Instruction fetch, first word	Supervisor data
Instruction fetch, subsequent words	Supervisor program
Halt	Interrupt acknowledge
Vectored interrupt acknowledge	
Non-vectored interrupt acknowledge	
Input-output reference	
Refresh	
Segmentation input-output	
Set bootstrap	
Reset bootstrap	

The Z8000 bus is called the Z-bus and consists of five individual buses: a memory bus, an input–output bus, an interrupt bus, and two resource request buses. As seen in Fig. 1.8a, the address and data buses are multiplexed. The MC68000, on the other hand, uses separate address and data lines. The Z8000 contains additional 8 pins for the segmented version. Compared with the 8-bit microprocessor, a 16-bit microprocessor provides a more detailed processor status for the designer. For example, in Table 1.III the processor status that can be monitored externally for both the Z8000 and MC68000 are listed. Bus control includes signals to separate byte and word accesses, in addition to transfer direction, and specification of memory or input–output. Bus arbitration resolves multiple requests on the bus. The interrupt signals of the Z8000 and MC68000 differ. The former uses three pins: non-maskable (NMI), vectored (VI), non-vectored (NVI), as seen in Fig. 1.8a. The latter, on the other hand, uses an eight-level priority scheme coded by three interrupt control signals (Fig. 1.8b). An interesting feature of the Z8000 is the multi-micro control input which permits daisy chain connection of a number of processors.

1.4   Input–Output and Communication Functions

In any computer design the interaction of a processor with its environment constitutes an important architectural consideration. At each stage of computer development and type of machine, different approaches have been adopted dictated by size, the application area, and technology. Large scale computers, mainly aimed at commercial markets, provided practically no facilities of input–output for the users to link their own devices. Minicomputer manufacturers, on the other hand, encouraged more user participation in fitting a machine in a given environment, in particular for process control and instrumentation fields. One manufacturer, Digital Equipment Corporation, in its PDP-11 series of minicomputers, provided a standard bus (UNIBUS) to which all input–output devices and memory could be attached. Minicomputer manufacturers very soon discovered that they needed to supply a number of standard circuits which provided the interface between the internal bus and external devices. These, like the machines themselves, were built using components of the technology prevailing at the time, mostly MSI circuits.

Microprocessor designers have all the resources that technology makes possible at their disposal for organizing the internal architecture within a chip, yet there are severe constraints when it comes to interaction between a processor and its environment. As mentioned previously, the available number of pins on an integrated circuit package restricts this interaction. The processor bus then becomes the crucial vehicle, providing the medium of transfer between a processor and memory as well as input–output circuits. Microprocessor manufacturers, like the minicomputer manufacturers previously, have also found out that in order to ensure the effective utilization of a microprocessor a number of input–output circuits had to be developed compatible with the particular bus utilized. However, they have mastery over integrated circuit technology which they could exploit to devise rather sophisticated circuits between the bus and a user device. The nature of this industry is such, however, that it is forced to reduce the different circuit types, although each input-output circuit type could be very complex, sometimes more complex than the microprocessor itself.

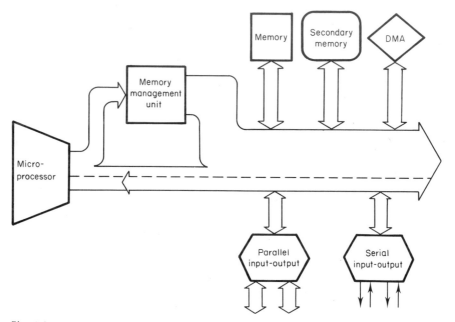

Fig. 1.9 A microcomputer structure.

In Fig. 1.9 we illustrate the overall structure of a modern microprocessor and the different types of ancillary circuits that are connected to the external bus. These circuits can be considered in the following categories:

1. memory (various types, RAM, ROM, EPROM ...);
2. memory management (only for high performance microprocessors, often an optional feature for large memory space);
3. microprocessor functional enhancement (floating point, real-time clock, ...);
4. bus control (direct memory access);

5. parallel input–output;
6. serial input–output.

In Fig. 1.9, note the particular shapes used for each type of system component. Where possible, this convention will be preserved throughout the text.

Bus protocol needs careful consideration to handle memory cycles or instruction fetch and operand accesses, as well as interrupt requests that come from input–output devices. To economize the processor power and bus accesses that are required, an attempt is made to make each input–output device handling circuit as autonomous as possible, with its own control lines (handshake) between the device and the input–output circuit as well as necessary buffer registers.

For the purposes of this section only the last two types of circuits will be briefly described.

Parallel input–output circuits

Parallel input–output circuits provide an interface between an external device which can supply or receive data in either an 8-bit or 16-bit parallel format. Some standard peripherals like keyboards are compatible with such a format. As shown in Fig. 1.10, in addition to a data line they provide handshake lines for control functions between the device and the input–output circuit. This enables data transfers to take place between the parallel input–output circuit and an external device independently, without the need of processor intervention. Data paths are normally called ports, usually being two ports of 8-bit width. Ports can be reconfigured to provide input, output or bi-directional transfers. This provides the programmed reconfigurability of these circuits, making them suitable for as many different applications as possible. Parallel input–output circuits also contain internal buffer register for temporary data storage.

Once a transfer takes place to an external device, the processor needs to be informed that the parallel input–output circuit is ready to receive the

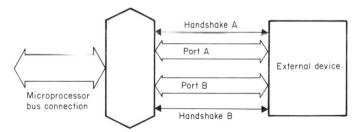

Fig. 1.10   Parallel input-output circuit.

next data item. In the other direction, if a data item is received from an external device it needs to be transferred to some memory location. Either case is handled normally by an interrupt. Thus the parallel input–output device contains enough logic to cause an interrupt and provide the information, such as an interrupt vector, as appropriate for a given bus and processor architecture.

For certain microprocessors the parallel input–output circuits that are available are very complex, including a processor and temporary storage (RAM) on the same chip, operating with an on-chip custom-designed ROM. One such circuit, the intelligent peripheral controller of Motorola (MC68120-1), provides a local bus where 8-bit compatible interface circuits can be connected. A double dual-port memory provides a buffer zone between the two buses, as shown in Fig. 1.11 [13].

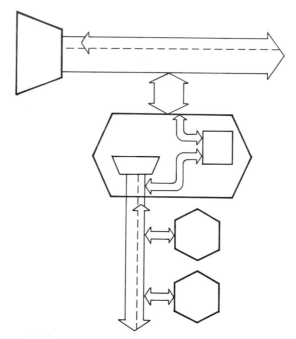

Fig. 1.11   Input–output controller.

Serial input-output circuits

Serial input–output circuits provide serial communication interfaces to external devices such as teletypes, modems or various communication channels. They include the serial-to-parallel and parallel-to-serial conversation functions, error detection, and a variety of communication protocols. The programmed reconfigurability feature allows for the handling of asynchronous modes and synchronous byte-oriented protocols such as IBM Bisync, and synchronous bit-oriented protocols like HDLC. The latter can be used to provide high level communication protocols like X25. In addition to a number of channels and their handshake signals, other signals exist to handle specialized applications like modem control.

Like the parallel input–output circuit, handshake and serial data transfer occur without recourse to the microprocessor, except when the internal buffer register becomes empty and needs to be filled with fresh data for the output or, conversely, it becomes full and needs to be emptied for the input. Normally in these two cases an interrupt-driven input–output cycle is initiated where the microprocessor starts executing the appropriate handler.

References

[1] Y. Paker. Trends in mini and microcomputer technology, *OECD Symposium on Distributed and Small-scale data Processing in Public Administration*, Lisbon, 19–22 March 1979.

[2] R. M. Davis. The DoD initiative in integrated circuits, *IEEE computer*, July 1979, pp. 74–79.

[3] W. L. Sumrey. VLSI with a vengeance, ibid.

[4] F. Flagging. How VLSI impacts computer architecture, *IEEE Spectrum (USA)*, **15**, No. 5, May 1978, pp. 8–31.

[5] S. P. Morse, B. W. Ravenel, S. Mazor and W. B. Pohlman. Intel Microprocessors 8008 to 8086, *Computer*, October 1980.

[6] The Intel MCS-48 Microcomputer family: A critique, *Computer*, February 1979.

[7] R. Sugarman. Computers: Our 'Microuniverse' expands, *IEEE Spectrum*, January 1979, pp. 32–35.

[8] Z80-CPU Technical Manual, Zilog Inc., USA, 1977.

[9] ZILOG Z8000, Specifications, Zilog Inc., USA, 1979.

[10] L. B. Pueto. Architecture of a new microprocessor, *IEEE Computer*, February 1979.

[11] E. Stritter and T. Gunter. A microprocessor architecture for a changing world: The Motorola 68000, *IEEE Computer*, February 1979.

[12] MC68000UM(AD) 16-bit Microprocessor: Users Manual, Motorola, USA, 1979.

[13] Intelligent Peripheral Controller (MC68120-1), Motorola, USA, 1981.

Chapter 2

Introduction to Multi-microprocessors

2.1 Historical Background

Since the introduction of digital computers in the early fifties, there has been a constant thrust to achieve more computing power. Each generation of computers, aimed at satisfying certain current requirements, have brought other applications to the threshold of computation, hence putting pressure on architectural ingenuity and improved technology for building more powerful machines to handle them, thereby leading to the next generation of computers.

Thus measures of performance have shown considerable advances in the last three decades. For example, the improvement of speed can be seen in the reduction of clock rate, starting in the millisecond range, then microseconds, up to tens of nanoseconds for many mainframe computers (12 ns for super computer CRAY 1), a factor of 10^5 in three decades. Similar progress can be observed in the increase in size and speed of memory and processor hardware functions so that more powerful operations are performed during each instruction execution cycle. At a given period when performance limitations of a current technology are reached, duplication of hardware remains a tempting option to go beyond the capability of a single machine. This, in addition to improved performance, is seen also as a means of improving machine availability and reliability.

Historically, to meet the computational demands of problems requiring vast amounts of calculations as well as time-critical problems, parallelism had to be introduced in varying degrees to the sequential Von Neumann machine. With the availability of low cost minicomputers the tendency has been to split complex computational tasks into individual components and to allocate separate computational resources to the constituent parts. The structure of many real-time processes lends itself to such an approach where the computational task is often geographically dispersed. The developments that are of interest to us here are in the multiprocessor computing field, where a number of digital computers are linked together to operate in parallel while communicating and co-operating with each other to achieve a common objective.

The idea of using a multiplicity of computers for improved reliability was applied at the early stages of computer development, e.g. PILOT, in 1958 [1]. "Polymorphic" (1966) computer is another example where a number of computer modules, buffers, and peripherals can be interconnected through a switching matrix which increases machine availability as well as improving processing power due to parallel processing and sharing of peripherals [2].

Array processors were developed for more special purpose applications which required sequential execution of the same instruction stream (mainly arithmetic operations) on parallel streams of data such as are needed to solve partial differential equations. SOLOMON [3] exploited this concept which then formed the basis for the construction of the now famous Illiac IV (1972) [4]. This is an array computer where a number of processing elements (64 built) are interconnected through a rigid two-dimensional mesh structure and are all able to perform the same instruction on internally stored data. All processing elements have independent memories. In Illiac IV the technology has been pressed to provide high speed, parallel, raw processing power (10^9 word instructions per second) which can be used effectively, however, only when the problems to be computed match the uniform and array structure of the machine.

More recent examples for such single instruction-multiple data (SIMD) stream array machines are ICL's series 2900 based DAP in the UK, which has about 10^3 very simple processing elements, each capable of bit operations.

The real-time computations, such as tracking of a missile position, impose a time limit during which the solution needs to be computed. If there are a number of simultaneous processes to be computed within the same constraint, it is very easy to exceed the capacity of even a powerful digital machine. PEPE (1971) represents one approach to introduce parallelism where each simultaneous activity is tracked by a separate processing element, therefore additional activities could be tracked by adding more processing elements without speed penalty. Overall control is vested in a host computer and associative computation methods are used to derive the particular information that is relevant to this application [4].

There are other schemes for handling high rates of data based on memory partitioning and associative memory techniques. OMEN-60 uses an orthogonal memory and STARAN (1972) employs an associative memory where a number of processors (64 and 256 respectively) simultaneously access operands in the special memory and perform operations on them [5].

A major research project at Carnegie-Mellon University resulted in the construction of the C.mmp machine in which 16 processors share 16 memory modules over a cross-bar switch. This has provided experience in utilizing such a multi-processor machine where an operating system and system programming aids have been implemented [6]. The Cm*, which was constructed more recently at the same university, is a multi-microprocessor system, based on DEC LSI-11, where the interconnection of computer modules is achieved by a hierarchy of parallel buses [7]. PLURIBUS is another approach for a multi-mini structure, where a number of processor, memory, and input–output buses are used to connect a multiplicity of such units [8].

With the advent of microcomputers, the interest in building large multi-computer structures has grown considerably over the last few years. To give just a few examples of work in Europe: in France, the Micral M of R2E; in the UK, the CUBY-M of Manchester University and the POLYPROC of the University of Sussex; in Germany, the SMS machine of SIEMENS [10], and others. Two main directions in research can be identified: (1) to build a general purpose computer by interconnecting a large number of micro-processors, and (2) to build a special purpose machine suited for a specific environment. In both cases interconnection for communication is an important part of the research. For example, the SMS machine utilizes a common bus for the communication of 128 microprocessors, each with local memory and memory space allocated for data transfer. Cm* has clusters of up to 16 microprocessors, each with a local memory, connected by a parallel bus and inter-cluster buses for communication between processors belonging to different clusters. Much work also is in progress for connecting a number of processors to a common main memory, as in the CUBY-M of the University of Manchester [9].

Another approach is a reconfigurable architecture where a multi-processor adapts itself to changing computational requirements. One such proposal is a network of low-cost computers (mini and/or microcomputers) linked with serial communication paths which can be reconfigured according to the needs of each computation, hence the name variable topology multicomputers (VTM) [11]. The proposed architecture is aimed at building highly parallel, large computer networks with a target of 100–1000 to satisfy a given class of computer requirement, especially in real time. Thus VTM can be placed, as a machine architectural concept, somewhere between a tightly coupled structure where processors and memory are shared and a computer network where several computer centres that operate independently are connected with public communications lines over long distances. An example of the former type is the Cm* machine, where a very large memory space is provided, accessible to all the processors, with the necessary buses and hardware to handle the protocol associated with memory access requirements, including protection and conflict aspects. There are many examples of computer networks where ARPA net is widely known.

The recent need to interconnect a number of various sizes of computers and peripherals, especially in an office automation and process control environment, has given impetus to local area network technology. A common communication medium is developed using coaxial cable or optical fibre where various computers, terminals, and other devices can easily be interconnected. The Ethernet and ring systems, which will be discussed further on, fall within this category. The DEMOS multi-processor system developed by NPL and SCION is, in fact, an example of the ring structure.

2.2   Multi-microprocessor Systems

As indicated above, to satisfy various requirements many multi-processor systems have been suggested and some built. One observes a variety of architectural approaches where processors are either custom built with multiprocessing in mind (including microprogrammed features) or they are standard processors with some modifications to suit a given multi-processor structure. When a multiplicity of microprocessors are to be interconnected, there are certain constraints that must be respected. Clearly one of the most important factors is the performance/cost ratio, where the cost of a standard microprocessor is considerably less than a custom built processor. While the cost is diminishing, as described in Chapter 1, the performance of a microprocessor is constantly improving. Thus the cost and full use of individual processors in a multi-microprocessor structure is not such a crucial design factor as it is for multi-processors. Furthermore, a number of ancillary circuits of considerable complexity are now available which can facilitate the building of such systems. Microprocessor manufacturers, conscious of the application potential of such structures, are offering special features and even circuits to help designers building their own multi-microprocessor systems.

A major constraint of a microprocessor in a multi-processor structure is the fact that the internal circuits are not available for the designer, however sophisticated, and all interconnections have to be done through the external bus. Only existing processor facilities can be used for the structure envisaged, with no possibility of enhancement.

It is interesting to note that, at chip level, the area of silicon that advanced technology is making available is being utilized to build multi-processor structures to improve individual circuit performance. For example, the 8086 design includes two independent controlled processors, running on the same clock but otherwise unsynchronized in their operation

[12]. One processor is allocated to run all external cycles (bus control), maintain the program counter and segmentation register, perform segmentation calculations, and maintain an instruction-stream look ahead queue. The second processor executes all instructions, resets, and interrupt sequences, maintains processor register, and provides data and addresses to the first processor. The two processors in fact provide a pipe-line structure, optimized with the help of an internal queue. Such design options, however, are only available to the chip manufacturer.

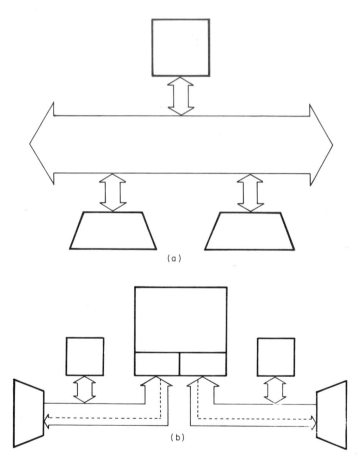

Fig. 2.1   Multi-microprocessor interconnection schemes. (a) Shared bus. (b) Multi-port memory.

A microprocessor with its external bus connections is, of course, an incomplete device and requires memory in a minimum workable configuration to make a microcomputer. When one talks of a multi-microprocessor, one has the tendency to visualize a number of micro-processors connected to the same bus which also contains a shared memory (Fig. 2.1a) or microprocessors connected via a multiport memory (Fig. 2.1b). The former requires resolution of bus control and contention when more than one microprocessor is linked to a single bus. The second type requires the design of multiport memories. Clearly in both cases memory is playing three distinct roles: (1) instruction and data storage for a particular processor, (2) temporary storage for data transfers between processors, and (3) storage of instructions common to several processors. In Fig. 2.1a the memory space shown can be separated through segmentation for different purposes, if this facility is available. In Fig. 2.1b the instructions and data which are local to a processor can be stored in a separate local memory so multiport memory serves only for data transfer.

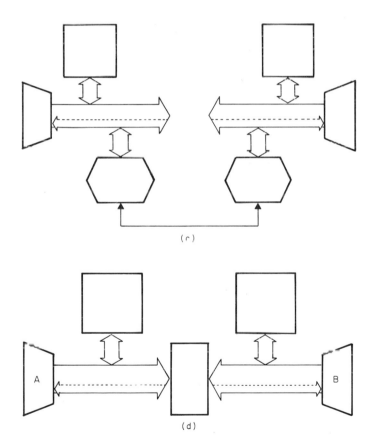

(c)

(d)

Fig. 2.1   Multi-microprocessor interconnection schemes. (c) Input–output linked. (d) Bus window.

There is a third type of connection shown in Fig. 2.1c. This is obtained when two microprocessors are connected via a parallel input–output or communication link. In fact the link connects two microcomputers each with its own local memory. In this case the interaction between microprocessors is achieved via input–output rather than memory access instructions. Conceptionally structure (c) can also be considered as a multi-microcomputers since the memory allocated and a processor combined constitutes a microcomputer. The execution of common codes, which is possible for cases (a) and (b), clearly is not possible for (c).

A fourth method of interconnecting microprocessors, is shown in Fig. 2.1d. This is the bus window where a given memory space of processor A is mapped to the memory of processor B and vice versa.

The names of the four configurations so far introduced are as follows:

1. shared bus;
2. multiport memory;
3. input–output linked;
4. bus window;

A multi-microprocessor structure can be built using the same type of microprocessors. In this case the system is called homogenous. If microprocessors of different types are used then a heterogeneous system is obtained. For interconnection either the system bus or input–output link is used. The input–output link can provide either a parallel or serial communication medium.

2.3   Multi-microprocessor Interconnection Schemes

In the previous section we have introduced a number of the basic structures used to build multi-microprocessor systems. We pointed out that, in such a structure, each processor is associated with an instruction and data space which makes it an individual entity (microcomputer). Whether this is done via private memory or a shared bus to some common memory is immaterial. A processor–memory pair is a basic functional unit, sometimes called a processing element, which can perform certain programmed operations. Each processor–memory pair, then, co-operates with other such pairs to perform a given task. This can take the form of passing data or performing certain control functions requiring communication between such pairs. The way that processor–memory pairs are formed, and their interconnections, could be changeable; such systems are called reconfigurable [13]. Thus, apart from the interconnection medium and its characteristics which affect performance, the underlying communication approach used is very important in understanding a particular architectural approach, its advantages and limitations, as well as options available.

In this section a computer interconnection classification is presented to follow the outline developed by Anderson and Jensen [14].

In building a multi-microprocessor system there are three basic components to be considered, as shown in Fig. 2.2a. The first component is a processing element which, in a minimum configuration, consists of a processor–memory pair. In hierarchical structures a processing element can consist of an aggregate of microprocessors and memories interconnected in some fashion which falls into one of the categories to be discussed here. The important point is that the cluster operates to perform a well-defined function and has well-identified communication links with other similar clusters.

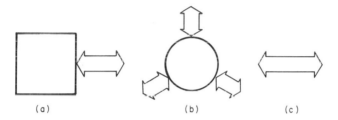

Fig. 2.2   Basic   components   for   building   multi-microprocessor   systems. (a) Processing element. (b) Switch. (c) Interconnection path.

The second component is a switch which performs an intermediate communication function such as routing. Note that a switch may contain one or more microprocessors. Since these are dedicated to perform the switching functions and are not available for general purpose computation, they can not be considered as processing elements.

The third basic component is the interconnection paths (transmission line). This could be a simple serial teletype-like connection, with 110 baud lines or faster synchronous lines up to 1 Mbaud or more. It can also be parallel input–output lines allowing the transfer of one byte or more at a time. The microprocessor bus can also be used as the communication medium. Asynchronous or synchronous protocols exist for digital data transmission. The actual medium used could have many variations such as a multi-wire bus, coaxial cable or a fibre-optic line. If such a path includes a public network, it is excluded in this text.

If a processing element is connected to a communication path, it is assumed that the processing element contains all the hardware and software to handle such a physical link, sometimes called a port.

A number of architectural concerns influence the choice of a particular system. The application may be distributed so that a well-defined function

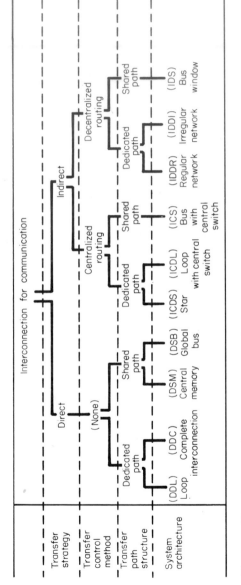

Fig. 2.3 Classification of interconnection schemes.

needs to be performed at a given location. In these situations the interconnection topology and the allocation of processing elements to certain tasks is dictated by application requirements. In other cases an increase in performance may be the major objective. In airborne computers reliability could become a major consideration. Another factor is system expansion (reduction). Certain architectures are modular and lend themselves to changes; others are more rigid.

Many architectural options that exist can be classified as decision trees, as shown in Fig. 2.3. The first consideration is the transfer strategy, whether a direct communication medium is to be provided between the processing elements or the exchange is to be done through an intermediary with certain operations at his discretion; for example, the mapping of source–destination processing elements (routing).

The second level of decision refers to the type of control method used. Here the direct strategy does not offer any options. On the other hand, the indirect strategy can be implemented either by means of centralized or decentralized routing. Centralized routing implies that all transfer mappings are done via a central switch. Decentralized routing, on the other hand, distributes this among many switches.

The third level of options refer to communication paths, whether they are dedicated (point-to-point between two processing elements or one processing element and one switch) or shared.

The fourth level refers to specific architectural implementation. Here we consider briefly the various configurations.

Direct Transfer Strategy Multi-processor

In this category of architecture no intermediary intervenes between the sending and receiving processing elements. Therefore, one processing element that needs to send a message to another element specifies the location of the receiving processing element and selects the correct path. A message undergoes no alteration during this transfer.

In this type of connection method the complete interconnection is an obvious example (see Fig. 2.4). The problem with this system is that the number of interconnection lines (unidirectional) required are $N(N-1)$ and the number of ports for processing elements are $(N-1)$, N being the total number of processing elements. Clearly for large N such an approach becomes impractical.

To reduce the number of communication paths required, an incomplete interconnection is possible. One such network, namely the loop, provides the minimum number of connection paths, i.e. one unidirectional path to the next neighbour (see Fig. 2.5). Since these paths form a loop, each processing element can communicate with every other one through inter-

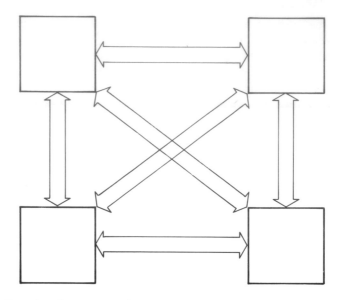

Fig. 2.4   Complete interconnection.

mediaries, the number of which depends on the position of the sender and receiver. A message is passed from one switching element to the next one until the destination is reached. There are several types of loops and some of these, like the Cambridge ring [15], will be discussed in Chapter 3.

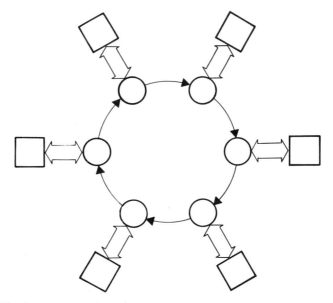

Fig. 2.5   The loop connection.

For complete interconnection, as the loop structure discussed, point-to-point dedicated lines are used. However, if a transmission medium is used in a shared manner certain architectural options become possible. The first one, which is called the contention bus (Ethernet), is shown in Fig. 2.6. A number of switching elements are linked to the same serial transmission path. If two processing elements attempt to use the path at the same time this is detected by both transmitting processing elements. In this case the message becomes corrupt and each processing element attempts to retransmit. Different strategies are adopted so that both retransmissions do not take place at the same time, thereby ensuring that the transmitters are not locked.

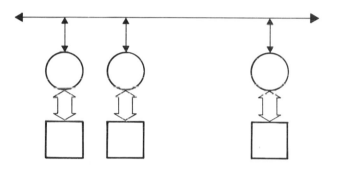

Fig. 2.6   Ethernet.

Another approach is to use a global bus, as shown in Fig. 2.7. In this scheme before a processing element has access to the bus it goes through a request procedure to ensure availability. Once the bus is allocated, no other processing element can have access to it. This is the so-called master–slave relationship, where each processing element has the right to become the master of a bus and hence delegate the other devices to the slave status. Such a system requires elaboration of the ways of dealing with competing requests and priority allocation. Some microprocessors include features to facilitate this. The global bus is discussed in more detail in Chapter 4.

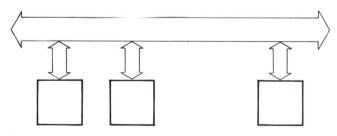

Fig. 2.7   Shared bus.

Memory can also be used as a communication medium. This can be done either as an extension of a global bus where processing elements communicate with the central memory via the bus (Fig. 2.8) to implement a mailbox scheme, or they communicate via a multiport memory (Fig. 2.1b). Memory as an accessible area for all processors to read and write as a means of message passing necessitates certain access procedures to be resolved either by hardware or software. For example, when one processor is updating a buffer area another one may be reading partially old and partially updated information. The issues of memory sharing will be considered in more detail in Chapter 3.

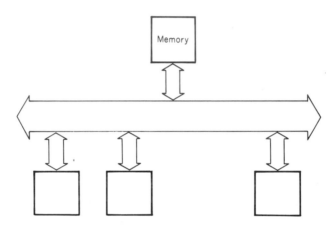

Fig. 2.8   Shared memory.

Indirect Transfer Strategy

For indirect transfer strategy architectures an intermediary stage exists which decides the mapping of processing elements. The availability of such an intermediate intelligence has fundamental implications about, for example, system expandability, reliability, and configurability. Such an intermediate unit could be a one-stage device which provides centralized routing or a number of local units (decentralized routing) (Fig. 2.3).

The star configuration in which processing elements are connected to a central switch via dedicated paths is one example (Fig. 2.9). The central switch contains a microcomputer where message routing is performed. A mailbox scheme is one way of organizing a central switch where a separate storage area is allocated for each processor communication. Mapping of logical addresses to physical memory is a way of changing the source–destination relationship (Fig. 2.9).

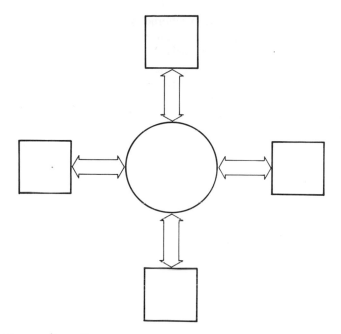

Fig. 2.9 Star configuration.

A loop with a central switch arrangement is another scheme whereby routing takes place at the central switch (Fig. 2.10).

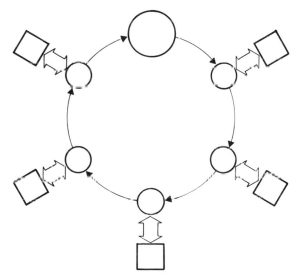

Fig. 2.10 Loop with central switch.

Figure 2.11 shows a connection scheme in which a common bus is shared by a number of processing elements. The bus transfers are controlled by the central switch which supervises all communication through the bus. The central switch normally contains a microprocessor. The SMS Machine is one such example where 128 microprocessors are linked via a common bus [10].

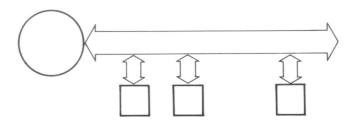

Fig. 2.11   Shared bus with controller.

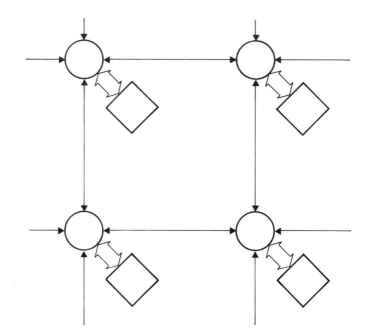

Fig. 2.12   A regular topology.

Decentralized routing implies networking where processing elements are interconnected via distributed switching by dedicated paths. The topology of interconnections is either arranged to suit the requirements of an application which might be regular, or to follow the geographical distribution of processing elements, which therefore is often irregular. A regular network topology is shown in Fig. 2.12. Such regular multi-microprocessor structures with fixed routing capabilities have applications in special areas such as image processing.

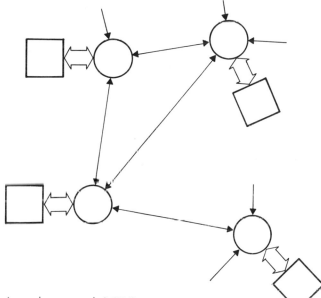

Fig. 2.13   Irregular network (VTM).

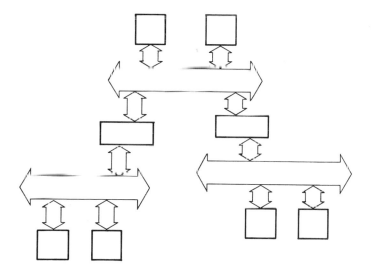

Fig. 2.14   Distributed routing and shared path structure.

An irregular network structure is encountered essentially in computer networks. One multi-microprocessor system called a variable topology multicomputer (VTM) falls into this category [11]. It consists of a number of switching units, each associated with a processing element. The switching units have a number of input–output ports which can be interconnected to form a given configuration to suit the requirements of an application (Fig. 2.13). Each switching element consists of a microprocessor with its local memory. In Chapter 3 more details are given on VTM structure.

A distributed routing and shared path structure is obtained by the bus window mechanism, as shown in Fig. 2.14. A well-known example which fits into this architecture is the Cm* machine [16].

References

[1] A. L. Leiner, W. A. Notz, J. L. Smith and A. Weinberger. Pilot—A new multiple computer system, *JACM*, **6**, No. 3, July 1959, pp. 313–335.

[2] R. E. Poter. The RW-400—A new polymorphic data system, *Damation*, **6**, January 1960, pp. 8–14.

[3] D. L. Slotnick, W. C. Borck and R. McReynolds. The SOLOMON Computer, in *Proc. IFIP 1962 Fall Joint Computer Conference*, Spartan Books, New York, pp. 97–107, 1962.

[4] P. H. Enslow (Ed.). "Multiprocessor and Parallel Processing", John Wiley and Sons, New York and Chichester 1974.

[5] S. S. Yau and H. S. Fung. Associative processor architecture, *Computing Surveys*, **9**, No. 1, March 1977.

[6] W. A. Wolf. C.mmp—A multi-mini-processor, *Proc. IFIP 1972*, FJCC vol, 41, IFIP Press, Montvale, N.J., pp. 765–777.

[7] R. J. Swan, *et al.* The implementation of the Cm* multi-microprocessor, Tech. Report, Computer Science Department, Carnegie-Mellon University, December 1976.

[8] A. K. Jones and P. Schwarz. Experience using multiprocessor systems—A status report, ACM computing surveys, June 1980, pp. 121–166.

[9] B. Aspinal and R. L. Dagless. Overview of a multi-microprocessor development environment, *Microprocessors and Microsystems*, **3**, No. 7, September 1979.

[10] R. Kober, M. Kopp and C. Kuznia. SMS 101-A structured multi-microprocessor system with deadlock-free operation scheme, Micro-programming and Microprocessors", North-Holland, October 1976, pp. 56–64.

[11] Y. Paker and M. Bozyigit. Variable topology multicomputer, *Euromicro 76*, North-Holland, 1976, pp. 135–170.

[12] J. McKent and J. Bayliss. New options from big chips, *IEEE Spectrum*, March 1979.

[13] R. C. Vick, S. P. Kartashev and I. Kartashev. Adaptable architecture for super systems, *IEEE Computer*, November 1980, pp. 17–35.

[14] A. G. Anderson and E. D. Jensen. Computer interconnection structures: Taxonomy, characteristics and examples, *ACM Computing Surveys*, **7**, No. 4, December 157, pp. 197–213.

[15] M. V. Wilkes and D. J. Wheeler. The Cambridge digital communication ring (Cambridge ring), *Local Area Communication Networks Symposium*, Mitre Corp and National Bureau of Standards, Boston, May 1979.

[16] R. S. Swan, S. H. Fuller and D. P. Siewiorek. The structure and architecture of Cm*: A modular multi-microprocessor, Computer Science Research Review, Carnegie-Mellon University, Pittsburgh, December 1976.

Chapter 3

Multi-microprocessor Architectures

3.1 Architectural Motivation for Multi-microprocessor systems

The progress of VLSI technology which made it possible to manufacture low cost, high performance microprocessors and other circuits has provided the impetus for constructing distributed computing systems using a conglomerate of such components.

The term distributed computing can have two different meanings. The first implies that a processing job is distributed among many processors. Parallelism is then assumed which makes it possible to identify the concurrent parts of a processing job and their allocation to processors which are interconnected in some way, e.g. by a common bus, shared memory, etc.

The second meaning of distributed computing is that computational tasks are distributed geographically. In this case the tasks are normally independent and individual processors, also geographically separated, could be allocated to execute them. Each processor may need to communicate with either a subset or all of the other processors. Their geographical proximity may vary from a few tens of metres in an office, to hundreds of metres in an aircraft, to hundreds of kilometres in a computer network. Local area networks is the term used to describe computers locally interconnected without the use of public communications networks [1]. Thus in this case there is a geographical necessity for processing to be performed in a distributed manner, whereas in the first case parallelism makes the distributed computing option possible. Again in the second case, it is worth mentioning that microprocessor technology made it possible to place the processing power where it is needed. For example, terminals are equipped with microprocessors so that certain local processing can be performed (intelligent terminals).

A distributed system as discussed above is also called a functionally organized system since each processor is allocated to a well-defined function either permanently or dynamically. The allocation of processes to processors could be done in a unique manner dictated by geography, or dynamically by sharing the load among the available processors.

An important application area for distributed processing is the management of data bases. In this case data is generated, stored, and handled in different geographical locations which also requires processing power to be distributed. Another version is where the same data base is replicated at different points so that it becomes locally available. Data integrity then becomes a problem [2].

We can identify the following major motivations for building multi-microprocessor systems:

1. to increase performance;
2. to increase reliability;
3. to meet distributed application requirements;
4. to build general purpose computers;
5. to build supercomputers.

Increased Performance

A primary design objective of the multiple microprocessor approach is enhanced system performance and throughput [3]. The reason for this is that the use of duplicated hardware should lead to better performance. This, however, assumes that the computational task lends itself to partitioning into smaller tasks where one processor can be allocated to the execution of each task. This is true if there is an underlying parallelism in the main application. This can then be exploited if problems relating to the identification of constituent parallel tasks, their allocation to individual microprocessors, the co-ordination between these atomic parts so that the ensemble operates efficiently, and many other related problems are resolved satisfactorily.

The most elementary type of parallelism consists of N independent and unrelated tasks (as shown in Fig. 3.1) which are allocated to N micro-processors. If these tasks are the same instances of a single task with different data sets, then to avoid repetition of the instruction code, a single instruction and multiple data architecture (SIMD) can be used (Fig. 3.2) [4]. Bit sliced microprocessors can be applied for building such machines. On the other hand, single chip microprocessors do not lend themselves to the construction of such architectures. A more common situation, however, requires that the parallel tasks communicate with each other; in other words, pass data from time to time. The frequency of data transfer depends

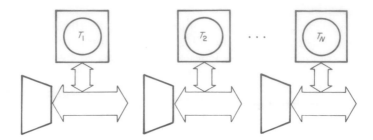

Fig. 3.1   Independent task allocation.

on the application and refers to the so-called granularity of the individual tasks that constitute an application [5]. This immediately places a new requirement of interconnection between the processors so that the data transfer can take place. The way the interconnection is provided and its speed depends on how often data transfer is required and how much data is to be transferred.

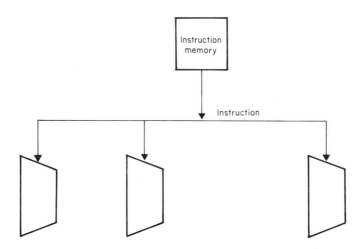

Fig. 3.2   Single instruction multiple data architecture (SIMD).

A different type of performance requirement exists when real-time systems are designed. This makes the execution time a critical factor. If the speed of a single processor does not satisfy the requirement then a multi-processor solution is needed. One such approach is the pipeline construct as explained below.

As shown in Fig. 3.3a, if a task T can be subdivided into consecutive tasks $T(1)$, $T(2)$, ..., where each task is independent of others and the output of task $T(i)$ feeds the input of task $T(i + 1)$ for all i, a processor can

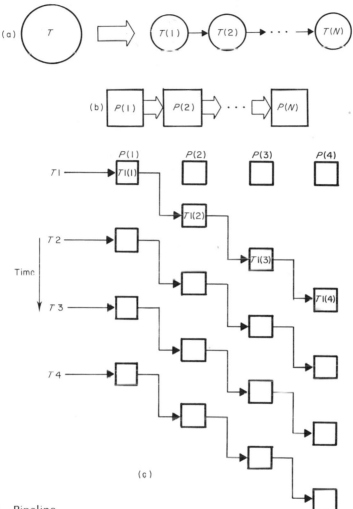

Fig. 3.3   Pipeline.

be assigned to each task where the processors communicate with neighbours
in a chained manner, as shown in Fig. 3.3b. Note that when $P(1)$ completes
the execution of $T(1)$ it becomes free to start the execution of a replica task.
This is illustrated in Fig. 3.3c, where four tasks are executed in a 4-stage
pipeline. In theory an N-stage pipeline, ignoring the effects of filling a
pipeline at the beginning of an operation and emptying at the end of an
operation, should speed up execution by a factor of N. This is rarely true
since the subtasks usually do not all require equal time and their completion
can also depend on input values. Thus the slowest link in the chain

determines the speed of the pipeline. Pipeline architecture is a concept much applied to building high performance processors for mainframe computers, and also for improving the performance of a microprocessor at the chip level. The concept, however, has not found wide application in the construction of multi-microprocessor structures.

To improve performance, another approach is to take advantage of the structure of a given application. The array machine is an example where processors are interlinked with a fixed topological configuration; this will be discussed later. If all processors compute the same tasks, such as those required to solve partial differential equations, then a central controller could send the same instructions to all processors. This is the principle behind ILLIAC [6], DAP [7], and other similar SIMD machines. As mentioned previously, microprocessors do not lend themselves to the construction of such machines. The variable topology multicomputer (VTM) (which will be described in more detail) constitutes an approach for building networks of microprocessors of a given architectural pattern which can be reconfigured according to the needs of each problem [8].

Increased Reliability

The motivation for increased reliability is due to the duplication of hardware which has now become economic as a result of the low cost of microprocessors and other LSI (VLSI) circuits. For example, if there is a bank of microprocessors which can be allocated to the incoming tasks, the failure of one microprocessor is not crucial since others exist to take on the job. There may be a loss of performance yet the system can continue to function (fail soft).

Reliability can be defined as a system's ability to function satisfactorily in the face of hardware/software failures. Thus the replication of hardware can only help the hardware failures at the expense of increased complexity since a multi-processor system which can handle failures is clearly more complex than a single processor system. This is a consideration which works against duplicating hardware.

A strong impetus comes for a reliable computer system when the vulnerability of the overall operation depends on the computer system's adequate operation. One example is the necessity of a "no-downtime" computer to pilot future commercial aircraft which are inherently unstable under human pilot control and reactions. In this case computers are as crucial to flight as wings to the extent that a computer failure is equivalent to a wing falling off [9]! For satisfactory service the computer reliability requirements are 10^{-9} mean frequency of failures per 10-hour flight. Conventional mono-processor avionics computers provide a figure of 10^{-2} to 10^{-5}. Chapter 7 will present in more detail some of the multi-microprocessor structures suggested to meet distributed application requirements for improved reliability.

To Build General Purpose Computers

The low cost and increasing performance of microprocessors have made multi-microprocessor structures an attractive option for building general purpose computers, with the expectation of making them more cost effective. Although there have been many experimental projects, the commercial advantages of such an approach have not yet been demonstrated for building mainframe machines [10]. There are several reasons for this. The main attraction remains performance. In a mainframe computer this is expressed in terms of millions of instructions executed per second (MIPS). This is normally obtained by the execution time of a representative mix of user jobs running on a system configuration in which the main memory size and input–output capability are well matched to central processor speed and user job requirements. Thus the temptation is to divide a required MIPS by a number so that the figure obtained can be attained by a microprocessor. However, such an approach does not take into account, for example, that data paths of mainframe processors are typically 32 whereas there are 16 in recent microprocessors. Furthermore, the overheads involved in co-ordination and communication between microprocessors are considerable. The operating system for handling a complex multi-microprocessor mainframe also adds its own overheads. Memory management too becomes more complex.

While there are fundamental difficulties involved in building a mainframe computer with microprocessors, the manufacturers are using these more and more for well-identified functions such as device controllers and intelligent terminals. This picture may change with the arrival of 32-bit microprocesors with powerful instruction sets and arithmetic capabilities so that, relative to overheads, considerable computing power will exist at each processing element. Memory management circuits that are becoming available are also simplifying the handling of large memory spaces that such systems would require.

To Build a Supercomputer

Here the thrust is similar to mainframe computers, the difference being that the objective is to build a computer system which is more powerful than the machines at the top end of available single computer power. Here, then, the cost element loses its importance when compared with the mainframe which has to compete with equivalent machines. Thus the idea is to have thousands of such components in order to supersede the processing power of the most powerful mainframe computer [11].

The construction of such a machine from conventional microprocessors and memory raises a number of fundamental problems. One of the crucial aspects is how to handle memory: multi-microprocessor sharing of common memory becomes useless beyond a certain number of processors due to bus contention. One can then design an interconnection method between memory and processor, such as a cross bar, which becomes very complex even for relatively small-size processors. Another approach is to use multilevel switch networks to reduce the complexity of an interconnection network. However, this leads to extra delay, due to the additive nature of delay at every stage. A hierarchical approach can be adopted where a cluster of microprocessors are built using memory sharing and the clusters then connected, again using a similar method for intercluster communication. The efficient use of such an architecture requires that the application is also structured so that parts of memory accesses are local and intercluster communication less frequent, thereby ensuring that a slower transfer mechanism does not reduce the overall performance. One such approach is the Cm* machine mentioned in Chapter 2 [12].

A different approach becomes attractive when a supercomputer is to be constructed for a special purpose, i.e. a well-defined problem structure. Array computers aimed at solving partial differential equations, such as weather prediction or picture processing, lend themselves to such an approach [13]. So far, however, the computing power of a microprocessor has not been sufficiently high to be able to compute the equation of a single node point fast enough to compete with mainframe computers. The availability of floating point processor circuits with the 32-bit microprocessors may alter this picture. To sum up, although the building of multi-microprocessor structures of 1000s or more units is an attractive possibility, neither technological progress nor the software methodology (operating system) have yet reached the level of understanding required for building practical, commercial machines. This is still a challenging area of investigation that will be visited many times over in the light of changing technology.

3.2   Factors Influencing Design Options

The design of a multi-microprocessor system necessitates the consideration of often conflicting factors. The hardware and software of such systems are normally complex. It is difficult to arrive at an optimum design to meet system specifications while avoiding both over- and underdesign (bottleneck). Table 3.I lists some of the main factors to be considered while building a multi-microprocessor system [14].

Table 3.1   Factors influencing multi-microprocessor design.

Topology	*Data paths*
Physical size	Concurrency
Local	Width
Geographically distributed	Serial
	Parallel
Physical interconnection pattern	Serial-parallel
Non-homogeneous nodes	Data transfer discipline
Homogeneous nodes	Circuit switched
Regular topology	Message switched
Irregular topology	Asynchronous
	Synchronous
Switch	
Centralized	*Deadlock*
Distributed	Prevention
	Avoidance
Memory (main/secondary)	Detection and recovery
Distribution	
Local	*Software*
Shared	Operating system
Hierarchy	Centralized
Addressability	Distributed
Direct	Database
Segmented	Centralized
	Distributed
	Reliability
	Hardware
	Software

Topology and Physical Interconnection Pattern

The first consideration is the interconnection topology which is quantified
by the size (number of processors) and the interconnection pattern. For
local systems, one perhaps has more options as to the topology whereas for
geographically distributed systems the physical location of processors and
possible interconnection lines often dictate the topology.

In the choice of the actual microprocessor, for homogeneous nodes all
are assumed to be the same. There are obvious advantages in this. In a
functionally organized multi-microprocessor if there are considerable
differences between the computational requirements then various types of
microprocessors can be used which leads to a non-homogeneous structure.

The interconnection patterns can be considered in two groups. The
regular pattern implies some basic rule, allowing the construction of
topologies of different sizes. A well-known structure of this type is the
N-dimensional cube or N-cube, which is shown in Fig. 3.4, for $N = 0, 1, 2,$

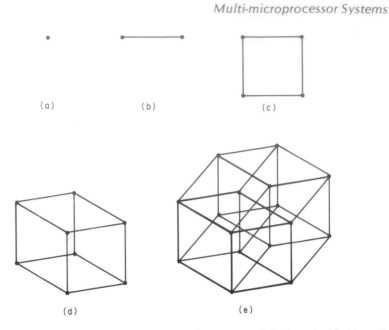

Fig. 3.4   *N*-dimensional cube. (a) *N* = 0. (b) *N* = 1. (c) *N* = 2. (d) *N* = 3.
(e) *N* = 4.

3, and 4. Note that to find the (*N* + 1) cube, the *N*-cube is translated in the (*N* + 1)th dimension. The number of nodes are doubled at each stage so that an *N*-cube has 2^N nodes and a total of $N2^N/2 = N2^{N-1}$ edges (*N* edges per node). There have been proposals to build general purpose computers (supercomputers) using this structure [15].

Another typical regular structure is an array type as seen in Fig. 3.5, where two- and three-dimensional structures are shown. In Fig. 3.5a the

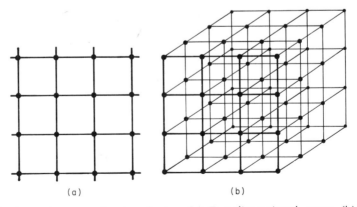

Fig. 3.5   Array type regular topologies. (a) Two-dimensional array. (b) Three-dimensional array.

nodes at the contour of the square are connected to the other side so that a closed surface is obtained. This yields a toroidal shape. The number of nodes is given by M^N where M is the number of nodes in one dimension. The number of edges is given by NM^N. Many simpler structures can be conceived to achieve a regular structure; e.g. taking a hexagonal mesh rather than a square elementary shape yields the structure shown in Fig. 3.6a. Figure 3.6 shows some of the interconnection patterns that can be used to build regular topologies.

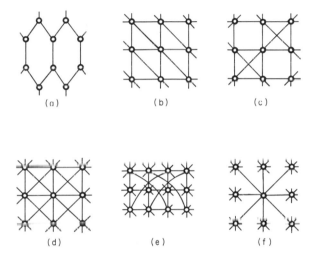

Fig. 3.6   Some typical regular interconnection patterns.

When a given topology does not provide a fully connected interconnection then either the application does not require that all the nodes communicate with each other or that the use of intermediate nodes are required to implement full communication. In the latter case the notion of average path length becomes important. This refers to the average number of intermediate stages that are needed between the nodes to provide full communication. Thus from node i to node j, if there exists a shortest path with $a(i, j)$ intermediate nodes then

$$\bar{a} = \sum_{i,j} a(i, j)/L \qquad (3.1)$$

where L is the number of pairs of nodes ($L = N(N-1)$).

For example, for the topology given in Fig. 3.7, $\bar{a}$ is $2 \cdot 31$ whereas for the topology in Fig. 3.5a, $\bar{a}$ is $4 \cdot 06$, both being for a 64-node network. In Table 3.II a number of regular topologies for a 64-node network are compared [13].

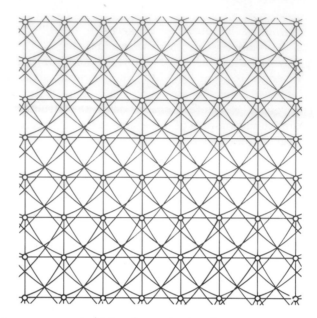

Fig. 3.7 A cross-connected 64-node regular topology.

Table 3.11 A comparison of 64-node regular topologies.

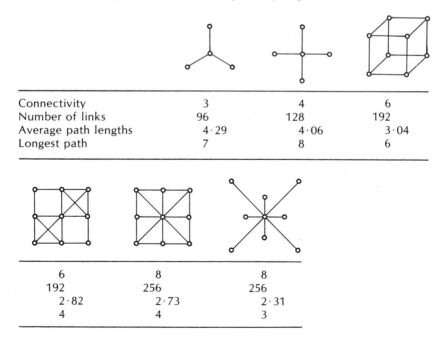

Connectivity	3	4	6
Number of links	96	128	192
Average path lengths	4·29	4·06	3·04
Longest path	7	8	6

6	8	8
192	256	256
2·82	2·73	2·31
4	4	3

Switch

The switch which provides the data exchange between several microprocessors could be either centralized or distributed. The various architectural options that this provides have already been discussed in Chapter 2.

Memory

Memory organization in a multi-microprocessor structure is very important because for many systems it provides the main link between several processors. In fact, for smaller multi-microprocessor systems this is the only medium where several processors pass data to each other. In a multi-microprocessor system memory can be either local to a processor, or shared among several processors. Often some memory is allocated locally to each processor with a common memory used for communication purposes. Such a structure clearly takes advantage of program locality where code and data belonging to a processor is kept in its local memory whereas less frequently accessed items, or items that are also shared with other processors, are kept in common memory.

Addressability refers to either direct addressing for small memories or segmentation techniques, as explained in Chapter 1, for large memories. Memory addressability is important since the directly addressable space of 64 kbyte (16-bit address) normally is insufficient space in a multi-microprocessor arrangement. Segmentation makes it possible to allocate some shared zone to several microprocessors and some segments accessible only locally.

Data Paths

Data paths are characterized first by the degree of concurrency, i.e. the number of data paths that can be used simultaneously. At one extreme we have systems like Ethernet, where a single data transmission medium is shared. At the other extreme is a fully connected network providing full concurrency. There are many levels of connectivity between the two. Shared data paths need to resolve contention (i.e. more than one processor trying to use the path). If the frequency of requests is high then this introduces delays, hence a deterioration of performance.

Data path width relates to throughput where parallel transmission is faster but requires more wires. It is perhaps worth mentioning that parallel transmission is used only in tightly coupled systems where a bus is shared among several processors. For distances of over several metres (beyond a rack) serial communication becomes more attractive. A mix of serial–

parallel transmission is sometimes used; for example, with byte-based communication systems where each byte is sent in parallel and sequences of bytes are sent serially.

The data transfer discipline to be adopted can rely on a circuit switched mode where a fixed path (temporary or permanent) is established between a sender and receiver processor. Such a path can be unidirectional only or bidirectional. The data transfer follows the established path which can go through a number of switches.

A second approach is to use packet switched (store and forward) discipline where data transfer is achieved by means of packets which include source–destination information as well as the data to be transferred. Such packets are injected to the communication medium where each switching point receives them and passes them on to the next switching point in accordance with some routing schema. Clearly the circuit switched mode lends itself to direct communication strategy whereas the packet switched mode is suitable for indirect communication. Synchronous and asynchronous modes refer to how a block of data is transferred. In the synchronous mode data is transferred in a continuous manner in step with a time reference (clock). Although these terms are taken from the communications field their extensions can apply here. For example, a direct memory access transfer can be considered as synchronous. Using asynchronous transfer the sender transmits when the data is ready. If a block of data is to be transmitted then this is divided into smaller units and each one then sent separately. Sender, before transmission, needs to ascertain that the receiver is ready and, following the completion of transfer, that the message has been received correctly (error free).

Deadlock

Deadlock is defined as a situation where no process can proceed without acquiring a resource already held by another process. Deadlock management is an important aspect in the design of multi-microprocessor systems since a number of resources are shared and there is a greater degree of complexity and interdependence of individual processes, as well as unpredictability in real-time situations. Deadlock prevention requires hardware or software mechanisms. For example, the circular allocation of shared resources can be implemented either by hardware or as an operating system function. Detection of deadlock is often achieved by means of a time-out mechanism. This involves the estimation of the time between an action and expected response (completion). If this time is not less than a threshold set previously then the action is repeated a number of times and if the response is persistently not received then a time-out routine is initiated.

Software

Software development clearly is one of the most important considerations in the design of a multi-microprocessor system. This will be discussed in more detail in Chapter 6. Here it suffices to indicate that the hardware architectural approach adopted needs to be reflected in the software approach. The first consideration is an operating system. This immediately implies a multi-processing environment, i.e. a number of concurrent jobs running at a given processor. The 16-bit microprocessors have features to implement this, yet if a number of microprocessors are linked together, the approach to be taken to develop an operating system becomes important. Either a centralized system can be developed where one microprocessor is in charge of operating the system functions of scheduling, resource allocation, etc. Another approach is a decentralized one where the operating system functions are distributed at each processing element site and there is no centralized control point.

Similar arguments apply to data base management. There could be a central data base with each microprocessor site maintaining its own local data base or the data base could be distributed. For geographically distributed systems the same data base could be replicated for easier local access. This creates a consistency problem when the data base is to be updated.

Reliability

Reliability is an important design consideration. Increased complexity requires particular attention to be paid to the detection of faults and to ensure system availability. As mentioned before, reliability could become the main architectural consideration, overshadowing other aspects like performance. Reliability must include both software and hardware. Chapter 7 will present a more detailed view of these issues.

3.3   Tightly Coupled Systems

When a number of microprocessors have access to a common memory space then a tightly coupled multi-microprocessor system is obtained. This is one of the most commonly used configurations which allows systems of limited size, generally up to 16 processors, to be built. Common memory provides a very fast data transfer medium as well as making it possible to share a common code. Although for small systems this provides a straightforward design, performance deteriorates rapidly as more processors are added. Management of common memory also presents software problems. There are four types of tightly coupled multi-microprocessor systems:

1. shared bus;
2. multiport memory;
3. bus window;
4. crossbar switch.

In this section the shared bus will be discussed in some detail as this is the type most commonly used and is well supported by manufacturers. The multiport memory and the bus window will also be discussed, albeit more briefly. The fourth system involves interconnecting memory modules to processors by means of a crossbar switch.

Shared bus

A shared bus multi-microprocessor system is built around a common bus which provides the vital link between the processors via a shared memory. Such a system is illustrated in Fig. 3.8. The bus used is similar to the microprocessor's own bus which performs memory read–write and input–output functions. It also has lines for interrupt handling. A shared bus provides a temporary link between two devices that need to communicate. The devices connected to a shared bus are classified as master and slave

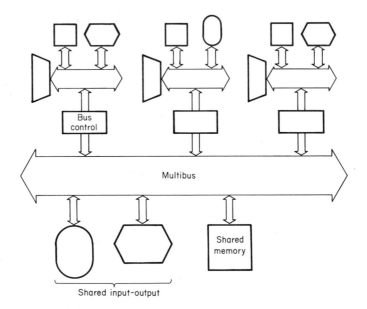

Fig. 3.8   Intel Multibus system.

devices. Master devices are given the privilege of requesting the shared bus and to communicate with any slave device. A processor is always a master device whereas a memory is always a slave device. At any given instant only one master–slave relationship can exist over a bus. Note that some input–output devices can be master and others slave. Normally a master input–output unit contains a built in microprocessor.

A shared bus must resolve the requests that come, in unspecified sequence and time, from many competing master candidates. This is done by the bus allocation (exchange) procedure. In Chapter 4 details of various schemes used for bus allocation are presented.

The shared bus system described here can be a very fast transfer medium such as 100 ns per bus transfer (10 MHz transfer rate with a typical 16-bit data path, 16-bit or more address path sizes). Yet it is easy to see that since a bus is used as a shared medium for all instructions (fetch, memory operand addressing, input–output operations) it is the main cause of bottlenecks for all microprocessors. A natural extension of the shared bus scheme is to provide each microprocessor with some local memory for its own code and private data, and to provide a common bus with shared memory and input–output devices. An example of such a system is Intel's Multibus system as shown in Fig. 3.8 [16, 17]. By manipulating address lines, local memory and shared memory spaces can be separated. Multibus provides up to 1 Mbyte memory space by means of 20 address lines and 8- and 16-bit data transfers. Data transfer rates of up to 5×10^6 transfers per second (bytes or words) can be achieved. The number of masters that can be connected is 16.

Performance considerations for
shared bus multi-microprocessor systems

Connecting a number of microprocessors via a common bus for increased throughput is an attractive approach. However, as pointed out above, the shared bus very soon becomes a bottleneck. Thus there are diminishing returns in adding more processors so that after a certain number each processor may improve performance only marginally. A simple analysis can be developed to determine throughput variation as a function of the number of processors [18]. Let us define Ts as a function of the number of instructions executed per second by the system. If no bus interference existed, Ts would be equal to the throughput of the individual processor (Tp) times the number of processors N. When bus interference occurs, one or more processors must wait for the bus to become free, reducing the throughput of individual processors and therefore of the entire system. Bus interference depends on how often processors need to use the shared bus. Bus utilization is defined as a factor b which is the fraction of available bus cycles required by an individual processor. This depends on instruction execution time and memory read cycle time. Typically b is between $0 \cdot 1$ and $0 \cdot 5$. The system throughput for $b = 1/3$ and $b = 1/10$ is shown in Fig. 3.9 (after Fuller *et al.* [18]). As seen in Fig. 3.9a, the multi-microprocessor system performance levels off after 4 processors whereas in Fig. 3.9b this happens after about 12 processors. Clearly, local memory plus common memory via a shared bus reduces the bus accesses and corresponds more to the model depicted by Fig. 3.9b. This model, on the other hand, does not include the additional overheads that exist when more processors are added. Thus the system throughput does not correspond to useful throughput. Nevertheless it shows that the shared bus multiprocessor configuration is useful for up to about four processors with no local memory and for about 10 to 16 with shared memory. The latter figure depends on the granularity of the problem, i.e. how often the individual tasks need to access the shared common memory.

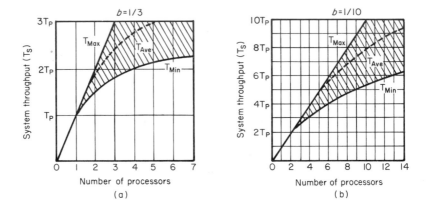

Fig. 3.9   Plot of minimum, maximum and average. Multi-processor system throughput (T_p = throughput of a single microprocessor) vs number of processors.

Bus Window

The bus window is a method used to interconnect two microprocessor buses, as shown in Fig. 2.1d. For a given pre-specified address zone the bus requests of microprocessor A are treated as bus requests of microprocessor B. Thus for this address space the devices (memory) of bus A are ignored and bus B acts as if it is connected to microprocessor A. This then gives access to microprocessor B memory located in a specified address zone. Thus microprocessor A can write and read the memory of microprocessor B or the same principle can be used to utilize the input–output devices. The bus access follows direct memory access protocol so that the link is developed only for one bus cycle. The address mapping is programmable as far as the target address space is concerned; the size of the window can be variable between two limits. For segmented microprocessors, the bus window segment could be given the right to read or write for both microprocessors. The bus window provides a very fast interconnection mechanism between two microprocessors with very little programming overhead. The disadvantages are that both processors needing to communicate must know implicitly of the existence of the window, its size, and location. Since the window space is mapped from one microprocessor bus to the other, it results in a loss of effective total memory space. Furthermore the bus window uses DMA accesses which means loss of overall speed.

The architecture adopted to construct the Cm* multi-microprocessor system uses a more sophisticated bus window method to interconnect more than two microprocessors [12]. Although the system was built using DEC LSI 11 processor cards, the principles developed could be applicable for modern microprocessors. The structure of Cm* is shown in Fig. 3.10a where up to 14 processors with local memories and input–output devices are interconnected via a common bus called the map bus. Each microprocessor normally operates with its own local memory. References to local memory are relocated in 4 kbyte page sizes and the switch provides the relocation tables. If an address is not local then the request is transferred, via the relocation table, to the K-map. This is actually a circuit which acts like a sophisticated bus window. It has the function of locating the microprocessor to which the address refers and initiating the appropriate

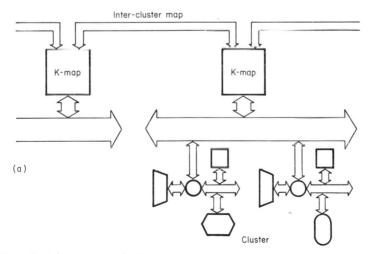

(a)

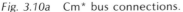

Fig. 3.10a Cm* bus connections.

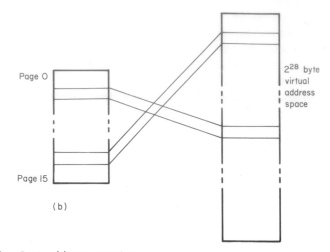

Fig. 3.10b   Cm* address mapping.

bus cycle. While this is happening, the microprocessor with the initial bus request is in the "wait" state. In addition to the addressing of other microprocessors' memories located in the same cluster (map bus), Cm* provides a hierarchical interconnection of clusters to an intercluster bus via the K-map (Fig. 3.10a). The virtual address mapping that is provided is shown in Fig. 3.10b. The total address space possible is 2^{28} bytes. For intercluster requests, however, queues exist so that a requesting microprocessor required for intercluster memory accesses is not kept busy for a long period of time.

Multiport Memory

As mentioned previously the multiport memory provides a means of interconnecting microprocessors where memory space can be accessed by several processors at the same time. A commonly used system consists of a dual-port memory which provides a link between the microprocessors. Thus data prepared by one processor can quickly be passed on to the next or instructions can be shared by both processors, avoiding duplication of code. Two processors can request access to the memory at the same time. Any timing conflicts are arbitrated on a priority basis. Shared memory, if used with segmentation, could identify some regions with independent read–write protection for both processors.

Dual-port memories are used for certain specialized applications such as the visual display unit (VDU), where memory is used for two concurrent purposes: to refresh the screen and update screen data.

Up till now the systems that we have considered are interconnected by mechanisms which allow one microprocessor to have access to the shared information, or other microprocessors' address input–output spaces by means of bus read–write cycles. In effect the microprocessor bus provides essentially the interconnection link and the bus cycle transfer mechanism for closely coupled systems.

Crossbar Switch

The crossbar switch is an extension of the concept of memory sharing by a number of processors (Fig. 3.11). Here a number of processors can have simultaneous access to memory modules as long as there is no conflict. The crossbar switch provides the interconnection paths between memory modules and processors, very much as in the telephone switching case. In such structures, however, a parallel data path is switched. As mentioned previously, the C.mmp has implemented this system using PDP 11 mini-computer processors [19]. The complexity of the crossbar switch has limited its applicability beyond a few research machines.

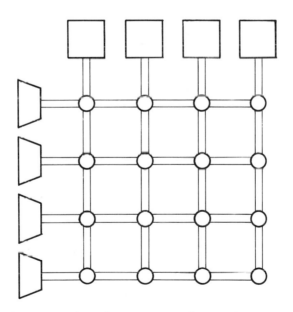

Fig. 3.11   Crossbar connection of processors and memories.

3.4   Loosely Coupled Systems

Loosely coupled systems are constructed when autonomous microprocessors with their local memories are interconnected via input–output
circuits (see Fig. 2.1c). Thus the transfer of information requires input–
output operations. Unlike the tightly coupled systems, the communication
medium is slow (1 kbit to 1 Mbit per second) and requires a number of
intermediate processes and thus overheads. The interconnection medium is
more flexible, covering distances from several metres to hundreds of metres
or more [20]. Beyond this is the domain of public communication networks
which lies outside the scope of this text [21]. Recently, computer networks
obtained by interconnecting machines in a given site, called "local area
networks", are gaining in popularity. These structures fall somewhere in
between long-haul computer networks and tightly interconnected multi-
microprocessors.

The interconnection medium for loosely coupled systems could be
parallel, where parallel input–output circuits are used, or they could be
serial, using serial data transmission protocols. There are also more recent
structures that can be used for building loosely connected systems. Here we
will investigate three such structures:

1. contention bus systems (Ethernet);
2. loops;
3. microprocessor networks (variable topology multicomputer).

Contention Bus Systems

As shown in Fig. 3.12, a number of microcomputers are connected to a
common transmission medium by means of a controller. This is a coaxial

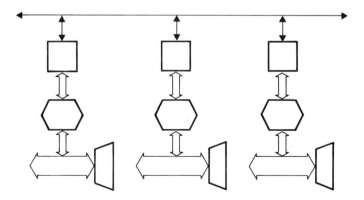

Fig. 3.12   Ethernet structure.

cable in the Ethernet system, developed first by Xerox and supported later by Digital Equipment Corporation and Intel Corporation [22].

The idea of packet collision and re-transmission was first developed in conjunction with the Aloha Network [23] which used radio waves as the transmission medium. Ethernet has the objective of connecting a number of computer stations (up to 255) as a local network over a distance of 0·1–1 km with transmission rates of 0·1–10 Mbit/s using coaxial cable. Further details of Ethernet are given in Chapter 4.

Each station, which consists of a controller and a computer (depending on application, a micro- or minicomputer or even a mainframe), operates totally autonomously the only link with the other station being the transmission medium. Thus when a station needs to send a message to another station it broadcasts a bit serial packet which contains the destination–source identification, the message, and an error-detection component. An indicator at the beginning and the end of the message is also provided. In order for the system to work, each station normally is in a state ready to receive a packet which might be destined for it. Therefore, all stations normally are in the so-called listening mode. When there is only one transmitter all is well while the remaining stations are listening and the station whose identification matches the destination receives the packet. If two stations attempt to transmit at the same time, or one starts while the other one is already transmitting, the signal on the medium becomes corrupt. Indeed this fact is used to detect that there is contention for the transmission medium, also called a collision. Colliding stations then have to re-transmit.

A major problem with the contention bus system is how to deal with the re-transmissions so that they are staggered to avoid stations locking in a perpetual collision–re-transmission cycle. Controllers in colliding stations each generate random re-transmission intervals to avoid repeated collisions. In a contention bus system control is then distributed and bus arbitration is randomly achieved. Each station is the same as every other station. When a station needs to send a packet it assumes that it has priority access to the bus. However, if it fails to transmit due to a collision, it attempts to re-transmit after a randomly adjusted delay which depends on the collision rate, hence the traffic, that it detects due to the rate of repeated collisions. Things are improved if a station first checks the bus to ensure that it is idle before sending its packet: carrier detection, in the case of Ethernet. In principle, for burst utilization, where the bus is idle most of the time, the contention principle works well. When traffic becomes heavy, the performance deteriorates rather rapidly.

Contention bus performance

Computer communications experience suggests that activity on a transmission line has a burst pattern of utilization, i.e. idle periods followed by intense activity. In a contention bus, a number of stations share the transmission medium. Stations, considered in pairs, may remain inactive for long periods of time. When two stations start communicating many packets start flowing between them up to the rate of channel capacity. The bus, however, is shared by the "burst" of transmissions between a number of station pairs. Therefore, when these bursts start colliding, packets need re-transmitting, causing a deterioration of performance. Taking the extreme case, all stations may need to transmit at the same time, in which case, if stations could be scheduled to transmit one after the other no loss of performance would occur since the channel capacity would be fully utilized. Since this is not possible and stations need to re-transmit following a collision, performance deteriorates. A simplified model for the Ethernet is used to derive, for a given packet size, a relationship between the performance in terms of channel utilization and number of hosts [23]. These curves are shown in Fig. 3.13. According to this study, for a packet size of 4000 bits, channel utilization is above 95% in the worst situation when all stations are queuing for transmission. Figure 3.13 shows the deterioration in the case of shorter packet sizes and an increased number of stations. This is to be expected since for smaller packet sizes the time lost by collisions and collision resolution becomes large compared with packet transmission time. These theoretical results have been confirmed by measured performance experiments done on an Ethernet [23].

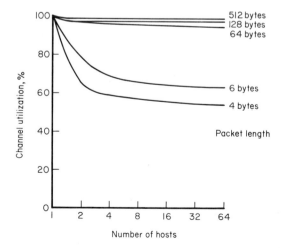

Fig. 3.13   Ethernet performance.

Loop (Ring) Systems

Loop systems were introduced in Chapter 2 (Fig. 2.5) as a means of inter-connecting processing elements requiring the minimum number of inter-connection lines. The communication path used for building the loop could be either serial or parallel. In this scheme data is passed from processor to processor until the specified destination contained in the message is reached. Thus each processor inspects the message received and checks to see if the destination matches its own address. If so, the message is removed and if not the message is passed on to the next processor along the loop [24].

The loop structure is easier to implement since it relies on message circulation by serial or parallel data transfers. Thus standard techniques to implement this transfer can be used readily to interconnect a number of microprocessors and serial or parallel input–output circuits. If serial lines are used then the serial communication protocols that are supported by the serial input–output circuits can be used to build the ring protocol. For parallel input–output circuits a character by character (8 bit) or word by word (16-bit) transmission would provide the basic unit of transfer to build more complex protocols. In this approach the processor checks incoming messages and establishes a match which requires time, thus slowing down the operation of the loop. Also no provision is made for a microprocessor to be taken out of service, which results in the breaking of the loop and the whole system becomes inoperative. Thus a loop, although simple to build, is vulnerable to a single link or node failure. To overcome these difficulties, a programmable input–output circuit may help to speed up the operation and a simple bypass circuit could be built to be activated when a processor is taken out of service.

Another approach is to build a special purpose switch (which could be microprocessor based) to handle the loop operations, as illustrated in Fig. 3.14. The first such system is called the register insertion method where loop messages are first stored in a register to check their destination (Fig. 3.14a). During the second cycle the register contents are transmitted to the next neighbour around the loop while the next message is being received from the preceding neighbour. In its simplest form the loop buffer is a shift register long enough to hold the message with additional addressing and control information, called a packet. More complex register or buffer insertion involves a first in first-out (FIFO) buffer at each repeater. When a node has a message to send it is first placed in the FIFO and the loop is broken to insert the FIFO as soon as the channel idle (or end of message) condition is detected. Incoming messages are then shifted through the FIFO until the original message returns, at which time the buffer is removed from the loop. Insertion of a new node to the loop causes a delay of one packet

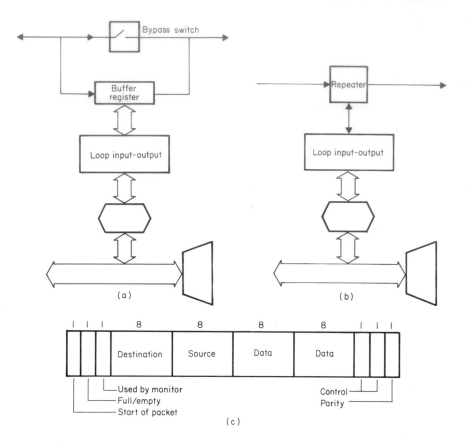

Fig. 3.14   (a) Register insertion loop. (b) Empty slot loop. (c) Cambridge
ring packet format.

transmission time. Since a special logic checks address matching, the
loading and unloading of packets to a loop is relatively fast.

In the control token concept, a unique control token is passed around a
ring. Any node may remove the token, insert a message, and append the
token. Once a message circulates around the ring to the originating node, it
is removed from the ring. Another system is called the empty slot loop
where sequences of bits sufficient to hold full messages are sent continually
around the loop (Fig. 3.14b). A node which has a message to send waits for
an empty slot and fills it. Normally a controller node is needed to ensure
that the slot pattern exists in the loop.

The packet format for a specific loop structure, namely the Cambridge
ring, is shown in Fig. 3.14c [25]. The repeater simply repeats the signal so

that delays around a loop are determined by propagation delays along the lines and delays introduced by each repeater. At the beginning of each packet one bit indication of the state of the slot (full/empty) is checked by each station. If it is full the address part is checked for a match. In case of no match it is simply ignored while the repeater has been passing the packet to the next node. If it is empty, this is again passed to the next node if the station has no message. Otherwise this bit is made busy and a packet is loaded into the system, including the source and address information. The control bits provide a means of handshake between a sender and receiver node. Parity bit is used for error detection purposes. One node on the ring, called the monitor, ensures the initial insertion of empty slots and checks for errors. A transmission speed of up to 10 MHz can be obtained in the Cambridge ring.

Microprocessor Networks

Computer network methods that have been developed for interconnecting large mainframe computers can be adapted to build multi-microprocessor systems. This has become a realistic proposition since the serial input-output circuits support low-level communication protocols like HDLC. As an example of a network multi-microprocessor a system developed by this author will be described: it is the variable topology multicomputer or VTM [26].

VTM networks

The objective with VTM systems is to develop methods for communication and synchronization among a multiplicity of computers such that flexibility is achieved to build parallel computer structures of a certain topology to suit the needs of a particular application. For real-time systems it is easier to identify the parallel tasks which are usually distributed spatially. Communication lines are provided between the computers dedicated to perform one or more tasks at a given location. The network thus obtained may be more like a star configuration. On the other hand, an array structure is more suitable for solving two-dimensional partial differential equations. For dynamic system simulation, assuming each computer is allocated to perform the computations for a sub-unit, a more irregular connection pattern with loops may emerge. Thus it can be observed that if parallel tasks can be identified in a specific application, then a network pattern can be drawn where each node corresponds to a task and each line represents the communication requirements between the tasks. For some applications the pattern depends on the way the parallel tasks are identified and interact. For dedicated applications the network pattern (topology) can be fixed, except for the possibility of expansion and for dealing with failures. Many others, however, require that the network topology varies with the requirements of computation at hand.

The main component of VTM networks is the node computer (NC), shown in Fig. 3.15, which consists of a local computer (LC), communications computer (CC), and inter-computer message handler (ICMH). The communications computer contains some local memory for routing information. The inter-computer message handler contains the input and output terminations so as to enable links to be established with other NCs. The message exchange between the local computer and communication computer is achieved by means of a dual-port memory.

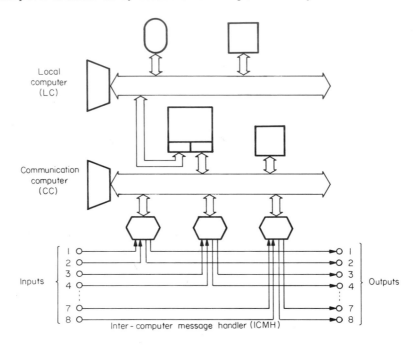

Fig. 3.15   Variable topology multicomputer node computer (NC).

Consider Fig. 3.16a where four parallel tasks are shown with inter-connecting lines indicating the communications requirements between them. Such a system can be implemented by a VTM network shown in Fig. 3.16b. Note here that each task has been allocated to one NC and one line has been dedicated for each communication requirement between two tasks.

VTM systems enable the construction of networks of computers where the topology can be altered at two levels: (1) physical, (2) logical. By

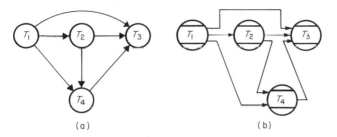

Fig. 3.16   Task mapping onto a VTM network.

establishing physical wires between various NCs a given network topology can be obtained. Thus connecting and disconnecting wires gives one the means of altering topology. This can be implemented by a patchboard for those applications where such changes need to be done frequently. The topology obtained by the NCs and the physical links between them is called the machine graph (MG). The topology required by an application is called the program graph (PG).

Thus, given a PC which satisfies certain constraints, a corresponding MG can be wired, as shown in Fig. 3.16. Over a given MG it is possible to establish logical links between two NCs with no direct connection between them if one or more intermediate NCs can be used for this purpose. VTM implements two schemes: (1) packet switching, and (2) circuit switching. The packet switching mode requires the determination of a routing strategy where each NC contains a routing vector to direct packets that do not belong to that NC. This is done on the basis of destination information contained in the packet, somewhat reducing the efficiency of message transmission. Since intermediate nodes are used, the time that a packet takes to reach its destination is also longer. Thus the packet switching mode can establish "virtual" links between NCs where there is no direct physical link. For example, from a machine graph given in Fig. 3.17a, a number of topologies can be derived where the dotted lines indicate virtual links. Figures 3.17b and c show how the same topology is obtained using the two different intermediate nodes, indicating the redundancy in the system. Figure 3.17d shows how a fully connected network can be obtained. If a machine graph satisfies the condition that it is not disjoint and all links between the nodes are bi-directional, then a routing matrix can be found such that by the inclusion of virtual links, the closely connected machine graph can be obtained. The management of virtual links is done by the communication computer and therefore it is transparent as far as the local computer's operation is concerned.

For block transfers, more effective communication is provided in VTM by establishing a circuit switched link which can be maintained up to the full

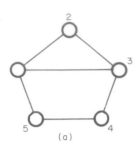

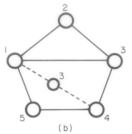

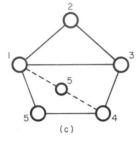

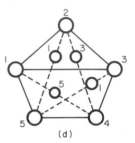

Fig. 3.17   Virtual links.

length of a block transfer terminated by an EOT (end of transmission) packet. Once a circuit switched path is established there is no need to transmit source and destination information, thereby increasing the useful throughput compared with packet switching. Notice that the delay time for both cases is the same, being dictated by the number of intermediate nodes that exist along a given path (path length).

One important point is that the circuit switched path, logically makes two nodes adjacent (neighbour) so that the source and destination is implied. This can be seen as the equivalent of establishing a temporary link between two distant nodes. To illustrate, let us consider a 16-node rectangular mesh VTM machine, as shown in Fig. 3.18a. Suppose, for example, a boundary value problem that has the geometry shown in Fig. 3.18b. To be able to "fit" the problem geometry onto the machine, we establish a virtual circuit path (VCP) between nodes 4 and 12 via node 8, and another VCP between nodes 8 and 11 via node 7 (dotted lines). This yields an effective (virtual) machine topology, shown in Fig. 3.18c, which now corresponds to the problem geometry.

The possibility of setting up VCP links introduces new neighbours which leads to the concept of virtual topology (VT). To illustrate, consider the MG given in Fig. 3.19a. By using VCP between nodes 4 and 1, 5 and 3, 5 and 9,

5 and 7, a star configuration can be obtained. This is a virtual topology that is constructed from a physical topology.

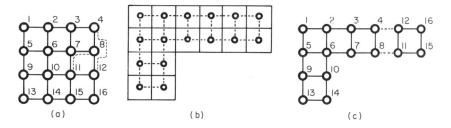

(a)   (b)   (c)

Fig. 3.18 Fitting problem geometry.

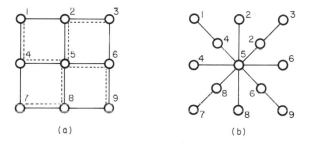

(a)   (b)

Fig. 3.19 Virtual topology example.

As shown above, over a given MG it is possible to obtain a closely connected graph, logically, by using a packet switched system, and virtual topologies by using a circuit switched system. It is convenient to conceptualize the different network structures that can be obtained from a given MG as "layers" organized according to their importance. This ordering is tied to a priority structure which is enforced when there is contention of a shared resource such as a link. Figure 3.20 illustrates the concept of VT layers. The highest priority layer (layer 0) is the closely connected topology (assuming a non-disjoint graph with all links bi-directional) where any node can communicate with any other node via the packet switched system. Layer 1 corresponds to the physical topology where only immediate neighbours can communicate. This layer is important in system initialization and reconfiguration. Layers 2 to 4 are user-defined. In Fig. 3.20, as an example, a ring, star, and triangular mesh topology layers are shown.

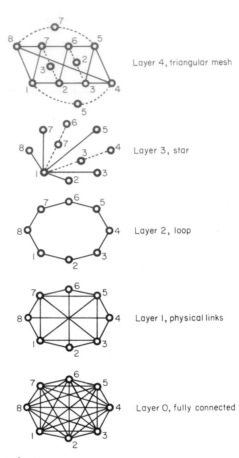

Layer 4, triangular mesh

Layer 3, star

Layer 2, loop

Layer 1, physical links

Layer 0, fully connected

Fig. 3.20   Topology layers.

VTM performance

Performance of a VTM network depends on many factors such as the characteristics of local and communication computers, transmission lines used, etc. Here we will not discuss the technology and application-dependent aspects which need to be considered with respect to a specific implementation environment, but we will mention certain fundamental characteristics of this type of network.

The VTM network exists essentially to satisfy the demand of transmitting a message generated at a source to its destination. A message originates either by a process or an external event. In both cases we quantify the traffic T_{ext} as the number of messages entering the network per unit time which need transmitting to their destinations (Fig. 3.21). Each message entering an NC is either terminated in an adjacent node or routed to a more distant

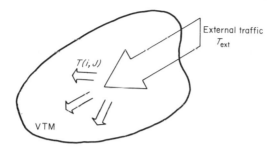

Fig. 3.21   VTM traffic distribution.

node. Thus each message generates internal traffic. This can be quantified as $T(i, j)$ which represents the number of messages per unit time going through the physical link (i, j) which links the ith NC with the jth NC. If the traffic input T is evenly distributed among the NCs, and for each message the destination node is equally likely, then the internal traffic

$$T_{int} = \sum_{i, j} T(i, j) = \hat{L}\, T_{ext} \tag{3.2}$$

where $\hat{L}$ is the average path length between NCs.

Thus for the same external traffic the internal traffic can be reduced by reducing $\hat{L}$. To reduce $\hat{L}$ implies either adding more lines, hence increasing the overall cost of the system, or using the given number of lines more effectively by choosing a better topology. The message transmission capacity of the VTM system, on the other hand, depends on the number of lines, $N1$, and the number of messages that can be transmitted per unit, time, C.

$$C_{max} = C.N1 \tag{3.3}$$

Clearly, internal capacity must exceed the internal traffic created by T_{ext}

$$C_{max} > T_{int} \tag{3.4}$$

which yields

$$C(N1/\hat{L}) > T_{ext} \tag{3.5}$$

Note that to cope with an input the factor $(N1/\hat{L})$, which depends entirely on topology or C, which depends entirely on the state of technology, must be improved. The former implies adding more lines and/or rearranging the existing lines so that the average distance between nodes is reduced. The latter implies faster transmission rate and shorter time for overheads.

The simulation studies which have been carried out for a 64-node network (Fig. 3.7) have demonstrated that in Equation (3.5) if T_{ext} exceeds about one-fifth of the left-hand side both the delay times and buffer length sizes start growing, making the network unable to cope with incoming traffic [27]. The topology consists of a toroidal shape where 64 nodes are placed uniformly following a Cartesian mesh which is closed at both sides. Such a ''doughnut'' multi-computer has a number of interesting symmetrical properties such as the possibility of shifting a subgraph in the x or y direction. By providing the cross connections shown it has become possible to achieve an average path length of $2 \cdot 31$, where the total number of lines is 512 and the connectivity of each node is 8. The maximum path length between any two nodes is 3. If instead of the pattern in Fig. 3.7d the pattern in Fig. 3.6d is used with the same number of nodes and links, the average path length then becomes $2 \cdot 73$ and the maximum path length becomes 4. Removing the diagonal links, the pattern in Fig. 3.5a is obtained where the number of links has been halved (256), resulting in an average path length of $4 \cdot 06$ and a maximum length of 8. Table 3.II (on p. 52) lists these figures of merit for a number of typical regular topologies.

The performance of VTM systems depends upon many factors such as the system specification, individual microprocessors used, communication medium and speed, network size, topology, and so on [27]. The dynamic and average requirements of an application, which are difficult to determine *a priori*, influence the performance evaluation. Some of the factors can be listed as follows:

1. System configuration
   — number of nodes,
   — network topology,
   — individual microprocessor used,
   — linkage between the local computer and the communication computer.

2. Networking aspects
   — communication protocol and routing technique used,
   — queue management discipline,
   — line transmission mode (synchronous, asynchronous),
   — the message format (fixed length, variable length block).

3. Application requirements
   — message generation frequency and distribution,
   — distribution of tasks amongst nodes.

Various performance measures can be used to evaluate a given VTM structure to meet a given application environment. The main ones, used also to evaluate computer networks, are as follows:

1. delay time;
2. system throughput;
3. buffer size.

Delay time refers to the time required for a message to reach its destination once it is generated during the execution of a local task. This time depends on the chaining of various stages to implement a protocol which may take several node hops, and the state of traffic of the system at the time when a request is made. Thus if a system becomes busy, a message may have to queue with others before a protocol action can take place, thus introducing further delays.

Average delay time is a good measure of a VTM system's performance for a given message-transmission request environment which can be specified statistically. An example of such a performance curve is shown in Fig. 3.22 [27], where IAT refers to the average message inter-arrival time when external traffic is assumed to arrive with an exponential distribution. Thus as the IAT becomes smaller, indicating that messages are coming at more frequent intervals, then the delay time becomes bigger. For IAT = 10 we can assume that the system becomes congested. For large IAT the average delay time approaches a constant value which is the minimum delay that can be obtained from a VTM structure with no queueing effects involved. As shown previously, this depends, among other factors, on the average distance between the nodes which is a purely topological factor.

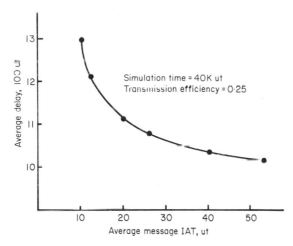

Fig. 3.22   Average message delay time vs average message inter arrival time (IAT). (The transmission efficiency is the ratio of the transmit phase to the synchronization period.)

Throughput is another important indicator of a system's ability to transport messages. A sample performance curve is shown in Fig. 3.23 [27]. Transmission efficiency f is a measure of the ratio of the time needed to transmit a packet to the period with which packets are sent. If the packet

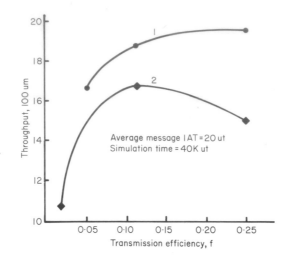

Fig. 3.23 Total system throughput in unit message (um) vs transmission efficiency. (1) External input is not affected by transmission protocol. (2) No external input takes place during transmission phase.

transmission time is assumed fixed for a given technology, then the larger the transmission efficiency the more messages per unit time can be transmitted over a given link. Figure 3.23 shows two cases. Curve 1 illustrates the case of a task which, when it generates a message, can continue execution when the message is handed over to the network. In this case, throughput increases as transmission efficiency is increased. However, the curve soon levels off, indicating the adverse effect of queueing due to congestion on throughput. Curve 2 shows a situation in which while message is transferred to the communication computer, the local computer is tied up so that the message generation task is momentarily interrupted. The performance curve in this case passes through a maximum then curves down for increased transmission efficiency. The reason is that the effect of queueing due to congestion not only reduces throughput but also blocks the message generation mechanism (task execution) which in turn reduces throughput. Such unstable behaviour is typical of some other multi-microprocessor systems, e.g. Ethernet.

Buffer length curves are not shown here. It is possible to simulate the average and maximum buffer lengths required when contention arises for shared resources such as a link [27]. It is interesting to note that as congestion builds up the delays increase and queue lengths start to grow so that, both in terms of excessive delay times and buffer sizes, the system becomes unable to cope with the communication requests.

3.5   Hierarchical Systems

Depending on a given application environment the requirements for building multi-microprocessors are varied. For large and complex systems a combination of different structures are normally used in a hierarchical fashion, rather than applying a single architectural approach in its purest form. For a system confined to one or more racks a common bus or shared memory provides a straightforward means of building multi-micro-processor systems, as explained in tightly coupled systems. If a geo-graphically distributed system is to be constructed, clearly serial links need to be used. Hierarchical systems can be constructed either using the same basic architectural approach or a mixed architecture. For example, the Cm* uses the bus window technique to construct clusters. These are interconnected to build larger systems using a sophisticated bus window technique. VTM, on the other hand, uses the multi-port memory technique to construct a node. Nodes are then interconnected by a network scheme.

An interesting hierarchical multi-microprocessor approach has been used by Litton Data System in the distributed processing system developed for military applications [28]. In this system the first level of interconnection is achieved by a shared bus (Fig. 3.24a) which enables processing elements to be built. These can be interconnected to form a cluster by means of a memory management unit. This means that up to 32 processing elements can be interconnected to 8 memory ports (Fig. 3.24b). Note that processing elements all have different size memories and numbers of individual processors. Finally the clusters are interconnected by means of a loop (Fig. 3.24c). The second loop shown is provided for backup purposes. A 20 Mbps serial transmission rate is envisaged. This type of several-degree hierarchy provides a basic architecture which can be adapted to vastly different application requirements. The size of each module is flexible. When the limit of a certain stage in the hierarchy is reached, the next stage provides the means of handling additional tasks. Serial interconnection levels enable geographically distributed systems to be built. Such systems are also more adaptable to changes in application requirements, such as expansion or contraction, as well as abrupt changes due to failures.

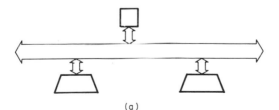

(a)

Fig. 3.24

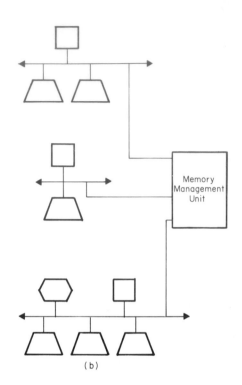

(b)

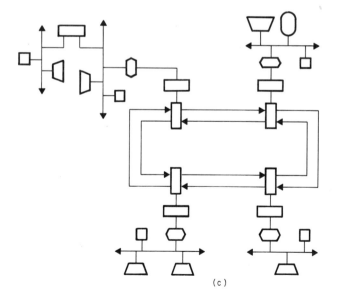

(c)

Fig. 3.24   A hierarchical multi-microprocessor system.

References

[1]D. D. Clarck. An introduction to local area networks, *Proc. IEEE*, **66**, No. 11, November 1978.

[2]J. Le Bihan, *et al.* SIRIUS: a French nationwide project on distributed data bases, *6th International Conference on Very Large Data Bases*, Montreal 1980, Proc. IEEE.

[3]G. Adams and T. Rolander. Design motivations for multiple processor microcomputer systems, *Computer Design*, March 1978, pp. 82–89.

[4]P. H. Enslow (Ed.). "Multiprocessors and Parallel Processing", John Wiley and Sons, New York and Chichester, 1974.

[5]D. P. Siewiorek and M. R. Barbacci. Modularity and Multiprocessor Structures, Distributed Systems, Infotech State of Art Report, 1976, pp. 401–418.

[6]G. H. Barnes, R. M. Brown, M. Kato, D. J. Kuck, D. L. Slotnick and R. A. Stoches. The ILLIAC IV Computer, *IEEE Transactions* **C-17**, 1968, pp. 746–767.

[7]S. F. Reddaway. DAP—A distributive array processor, *1st Annual Symposium on Computer Architecture*, Florida, 1974.

[8] Y. Paker and M. Bozyigit. Variable topology multicomputer, *EUROMICRO 76*, North Holland, 1976, pp. 135–140.

[9] R. Bernard. The 'no-downtime' computer, *IEEE Spectrum*, September 1980.

[10] G. Tjaden and M. Cohen. "Some consideration in the design of mainframe processor with microprocessor technology", *IEEE Computer*, August, 1979, pp. 68–73.

[11] C. R. Vick, S. P. Kartastev and S. I. Kartastev. Adaptable architecture for supersystems, *IEEE Computer*, November 1980.

[12] R. J. Swan, S. H. Fuller and D. P. Siewiorek. Cm*: a modular multi-microprocessor, Carnegie Mellon University, November 1976.

[13] Y. Paker and M. Bozyigit. Array type variable topology multicomputer systems, *Proc. 1977 Int. Conference on Parallel Processing*, Wayne State University, Jean-Loup Baer, Ed., 1977.

[14] D. P. Siewiorek. Modularity and multi-microprocessor structures, *Proc. 7th Annual Workshop on Microprogramming*, Palo Alto, California, October 1974, pp. 186–193.

[15] H. Sullivan and T. Bashkow. A large scale, homogeneous, fully distributed parallel machine, *Comp. Arch. News*, **5**, March 1977.

[16] Intel Multibus specification, Intel Corporation, Santa Clara, California, USA, 1978.

[17] G. Tr. Reyling. Performance and control of multiple microprocessor systems, *Computer Design*, March 1974.

[18] S. H. Fuller, J. Ousterhont, L. Raskin, P. Robinfeld, P. Sindhn and R. Swan. Multi-microprocessors: an overview and working example, *Proc. IEEE*, **66**, No. 2, February 1978, pp. 216–228.

[19] W. A. Wulf and C. G. Bell. C.mmp—A multi-mini-processor, *Fall Joint Computer Conference*, 1972, pp. 756–777.

[20] W. L. Spetz. Microprocessor networks, *IEEE Computer*, July 1977.

[21] N. Abramson and F. F. Kuo. "Computer Communication Networks", Prentice-Hall, New Jersey, 1975.

[22] R. M. Metcalfe and D. R. Boggs. Ethernet: distributed packet switching for local computer networks, *Comm. ACM*, **19**, No. 7, July 1976.

[23] J. F. Shoch and J. A. Hupp. Measured performance of an Ethernet Local
     Network, *Local Area Communications Network Symposium*, Mitre Corp. and
     National Bureau of Standards, Boston, May 1979.
[24] M. V. Wilkes and D. J.Wheeler. The Cambridge digital communication ring,
     Local Area Communication Networks Symposium, Mitre Corp. and National
     Bureau of Standards, Boston, May 1979.
[25] A. Hopper. The Cambridge ring—A local network, in "Advanced Techniques
     for Microprocessor Systems", Ed. F. K. Hanna, Peter Perigrinus Ltd., 1980.
[26] Y. Paker. Variable topology multicomputer system evaluation, US European
     Research Office, Grant No. 37-36-0401, November 1976.
[27] M. Bozyigit. A dense variable topology multicomputer system: specifications
     and performance analysis, Polytechnic of Central London, Ph.D. Thesis, 1979.
[28] R. Mauniello. A distributed processing system for military applications, Part 1:
     System overview, *Computer Design*, September 1980, pp. 14–30.

Chapter 4

Interconnection and Communication

4.1 Introduction

In the design and construction of multi-microprocessor systems, the inter-connection and communication scheme used remains a crucial architectural decision which affects both the hardware structure and the software system. A number of options are available to the designer depending on the size, topology, and performance of the system, and the individual micro-processors used. A hierarchical combination of interconnection mechanisms is possible, particularly when building larger systems. In this chapter the main interconnection schemes currently used for building multi-microprocessor systems will be discussed. The first system to be considered is the parallel bus, which utilizes the external bus of a microprocessor or its extension as the main transmission medium. Such a bus system can operate with a 10 MHz clock transmitting 16-bit addresses and 8-bit bytes or 16-bit words in parallel. A serial bus provides a single line interconnecting medium operating with speeds of 1–10 Mbytes per second. The contention bus has already been introduced which enables connections to be made to a common transmission line (normally a coaxial line) by means of controllers. Finally, point-to-point communication can be implemented, a direct transmission line between two microcomputers being the interconnection medium. The techniques used, then, are similar to those applied in computer communications networks where store-forward and routing provides the means of communication between the microprocessors not immediately linked.

4.2 Parallel Bus Structures

In the application of microprocessors, the external bus assumes primary importance. It provides the only means of access to a processor and a transmission medium, allowing the connection of a memory and a wide variety of devices. The external bus has become a key element providing a basis for standardization. Thus we observe each manufacturer trying to develop its own standards like the multibus of Intel [1] and the Z-bus of Zilog [2]. The idea of developing a parallel bus standard as the medium enabling connection of a variety of external devices goes back to 1970, when Digital Equipment Corporation introduced the UNIBUS for their PDP-11 series of machines. In addition to the manufacturers trying to develop their own standards compatible within their own product lines, efforts have been made to develop more universal standards. Thus the IEEE 488 bus is an early attempt at a communication standard for instrumentation applications.

The standards developed specifically for microprocessors include the S-100 bus [3] and the proposed IEEE 796 bus standard [4]. In this section we will discuss the utilization of a parallel bus for building multi-microprocessor systems. The presentation will be based on Intel's multibus and the proposed IEEE 796 standard. Only functional features relevant to multi-microprocessor configurations will be emphasized, without going into full details of aspects such as electrical timings and mechanical features.

Bus Signals

The main purpose of a parallel bus is to provide a transmission mechanism between a processor memory and a processor input–output device. Normally the memory space and input–output address space are distinct, which implies differentiation between different types of transmission requests generated by an input–output device, the so-called event driven input–output. Finally, since a parallel bus is a shared transmission medium, its exclusive use at any given moment needs to be ensured.

As shown in Fig. 4.1, a parallel bus has the following class of lines (signals):

1. address lines;
2. data lines;
3. control lines;
4. interrupt lines;
5. bus exchange lines.

Address lines specify the address of a memory location or a referenced input–output device. The IEEE 796 bus allows 20 address lines for about 1 Mbyte (1 048 576 bytes) memory locations. The input–output address space is restricted to 16 address lines or 64 K devices. In this case the top four address lines are ignored.

Data lines are used to carry information to and from a memory location

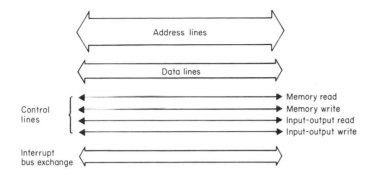

Fig. 4.1 Parallel bus signals.

or an input–output device specified by address lines. Depending on whether one is using an 8- or 16-bit system, there are 8 or 16 data lines.

Control lines are used to implement the actual bus transfers. For memory a read and a write operation is differentiated by means of the control lines. Similarly input–output transfers are implemented by separate control lines which also indicate the direction of a transfer (read or write). The control lines also serve to indicate the validity of signals on the address on data lines. To complete a data transfer cycle, an acknowledge line exists to indicate to the device which is forcing a transfer, the so-called master, that the operation has been completed. The acknowledge line is activated by the subservient device, the so-called slave. Under the category of control lines other signals can be combined such as a constant clock, a bus clock, and initialize.

Interrupt lines are provided to implement event-driven input–output operations. For this purpose a number of interrupt request lines, eight for the IEEE 796, exist where an input–output initiates an interrupt handling cycle. Each line corresponds to a different priority level, thus making it possible for concurrent interrupt requests to originate where the highest priority one is honoured. Interrupt requests normally can be nested. The interrupt acknowledge line is used to indicate to the device that its request has been accepted. In this case if the interrupt requires transfer on an interrupt vector then the transfer cycle is initiated for the vector to be transmitted from the input–output device to the processor. A non-bus vectored interrupt, on the other hand, does not require such a transfer.

Bus exchange lines allow several masters to share the bus so that they can communicate with slaves in an exclusive manner. To implement this the IEEE 796 proposes the following signals [4]:

1. bus clock;
2. bus busy;

3. bus priority out;
4. bus request;
5. common bus request.

These signals will be described briefly.

1. Bus clock. This periodic clock signal is used to synchronize the exchange logic. A maximum frequency of 10 MHz is specified. This frequency can be slowed, stepped or stopped by system design.
2. Bus busy. This signal is driven by the master in control of the bus. All other masters monitor this signal to determine the state of the bus. The bus clock synchronizes this signal.
3. Bus priority out. This signal, when activated by a bus master, indicates to the bus master of the next lower priority that it may gain control of the bus. This signal is used only for daisy-chained serial priority resolution.
4. Bus request. The bus request line is used with the parallel priority resolution scheme where it indicates a request for the bus. A parallel arbiter then selects the request with the highest priority by activating the bus priority input of that master.
5. Common bus request. Any master that wants control of the bus, but does not control it, can activate this signal. This indicates while a master is in possession of the bus whether there are other masters requesting the bus.

Bus Arbitration

Bus arbitration is an important aspect in implementing shared bus structures. When a number of master candidates are sharing a common bus and one requires the use of the bus (Fig. 4.2), the first step is to check if the bus is available. This is done normally by a signal line, which is connected to all masters and can be interrogated by the candidate master (Fig. 4.3). As soon as the bus is found to be free then the master candidate indicates to the system its intention to use the bus. This is done by a bus request signal which is fed to an arbiter which has to resolve competing requests for the bus. Once the bus is allocated, this is indicated to the master candidate with a bus acknowledge signal. The declared master forces the signal on bus busy line to busy state. The master then can initiate a bus cycle to perform a memory or input–output operation. Once the operation is completed, the master sets the bus busy line to free state. This operation is shown in Fig. 4.4.

Many arbiter schemes are possible to ensure equitable utilization of the bus by a number of competing masters. It is important to ensure that there

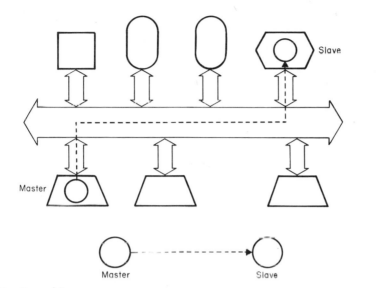

Fig. 4.2 Shared bus.

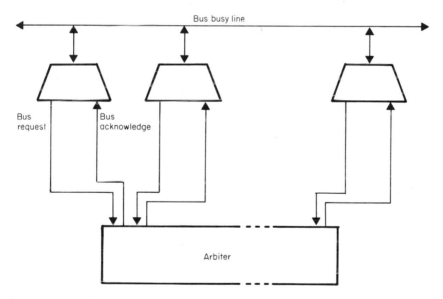

Fig. 4.3 Bus arbitration.

is no starvation (i.e. some masters never having a chance to access the bus). The arbiter also needs to be given a basis for choosing when there are a number of simultaneous requests. This then involves building a priority scheme into the arbiter. Some arbiter methods are indicated below.

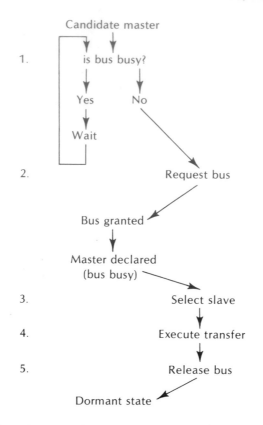

Fig. 4.4   Bus allocation procedure.

A round-robin arbiter polls each master one after the other in a given circular sequence (round-robin) (Fig. 4.5a). In such a rotating priority-resolving technique all microprocessors can be assumed of the same priority level. They are placed in a circular fashion where a pointer is stepped through each time there is a transfer request. The request of the microprocessor that is reached first by the pointer is honoured first. The pointer then starts from that position next time there is a request. The implementation of the rotating priority-resolving technique is very much like the parallel priority-resolving technique introduced below where the encoder–decoder circuit is replaced by a shift register and some additional logic.

A more commonly used system is to allocate a fixed priority to each processor. This can be done using a serial (daisy chain) scheme (Fig. 4.5b) or a parallel priority scheme (Fig. 4.5c).

To implement the serial priority scheme each processor (master) is

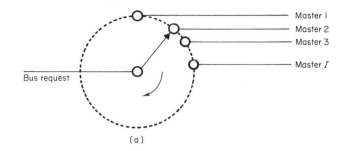

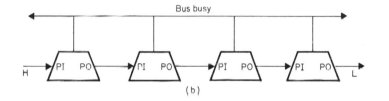

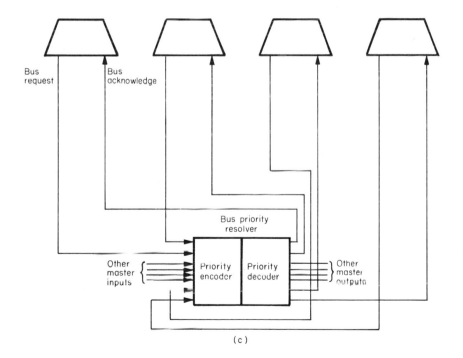

Fig. 4.5 Bus arbitration techniques. (a) Round-robin arbitration. (b) Serial bus arbitration. (c) Parallel bus arbitration.

equipped with an input called priority input (PI) and an output called priority output (PO). These are connected to form a chain as illustrated in Fig. 4.5c. The leftmost master PI input is connected to logic high (H). The priority of each master depends on its position along the chain where the leftmost master has the highest priority.

Normally, the leftmost high logic level (H) is propagated through each processor to the right, which indicates to each master that no master of higher priority is currently requesting the bus. In this situation a master can request the bus by forcing its PO output to logic low state which indicates to the rightmost master that the bus is busy. This is propagated to the right up to the rightmost master so that they all are made aware of a pending request by a high priority master. Bus busy line is used to signal to the high priority master interrupting a lower priority master the acknowledgement of the request. Therefore, a higher priority master does not start transmission until the bus busy signal goes down. The serial priority scheme has the advantage that it does not require additional arbiter logic. Some micro-processors already have the associated logic incorporated (like the Z8000). The disadvantage is that the arbitration time depends on the length of the chain. For example, if we assume a 50 ns gate delay time between PI and PO, then for a ten-master chain it will take 500 ns for the first master's request to be known to the last master in the chain.

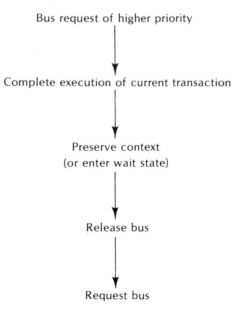

Fig. 4.6   Bus pre-emption.

For faster resolution of bus arbitration, a parallel priority resolver circuit can be used. This is shown in Fig. 4.5c. This circuit continuously checks the bus requests and when a number of requests arrive simultaneously it activates the master with highest priority. The speed of this circuit does not depend on the number of masters. For an eight-master system arbitration takes about 40 ns.

When a processor captures the bus, if another processor with higher priority requests it then it is forced to release the bus. Before doing this, however, it needs to preserve its context and enter a wait state and can then release the bus. We show the sequence of events in Fig. 4.6.

In cases where the current transaction is understood as a single transfer (memory or input–output), the interrupt by a higher priority master may not be desirable until a control section is executed. To achieve this certain multi-microprocessor systems provide a bus lock function, where the busy line is kept high regardless of requests from a higher priority master. As soon as the control section, like test and set instruction execution, is completed the bus is unlocked.

Intel's Bus Arbiter Circuit

To illustrate how the bus exchange mechanism can be used to implement a multi-microprocessor system and the several options available, we will consider the use of Intel's bus arbiter circuit [5]. This circuit (Fig. 4.7) is used in conjunction with a bus controller that generates memory and input–output signals to interface the microprocessors to a common parallel bus (in this case the multibus), as shown in Fig. 4.8. A microprocessor operates as if the bus arbiter and the associated circuits did not exist. Thus each microprocessor requests the bus as if it had the exclusive use of it. If, however, the bus is occupied by another microprocessor of higher priority then no transfer acknowledgement is returned and the requesting microprocessor enters into a wait state. In other words, the microprocessor extends its transfer cycle until the bus becomes free and its request is executed and an acknowledgement is returned.

In the circuit shown in Fig. 4.9, if there are several concurrent requests, only one signal corresponding to the request with the highest priority is activated. Thus each priority encoder–decoder output is connected to the bus priority input of a bus arbiter. As soon as one microprocessor has been selected, it can not assert its transfer cycle until the bus is released. The bus busy signal makes it possible to determine the state of the bus. The advantage of this scheme is that arbitration is very fast, the disadvantage is that an additional encoder–decoder circuit is needed.

The serial priority-resolving technique eliminates the necessity of extra hardware. The microprocessors are ordered in sequence of their relative

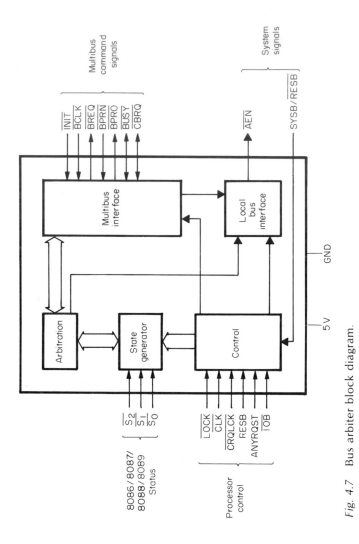

Fig. 4.7 Bus arbiter block diagram.

priority and the bus arbiter circuit of each one is interconnected following this sequence, as shown in Fig. 4.10. The BPRN* input of the highest priority bus arbiter is grounded. Note that in an idle state, this input is

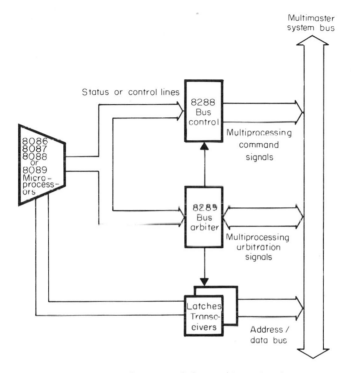

Fig. 4.8   Multi-microprocessor design with bus arbiter circuit.

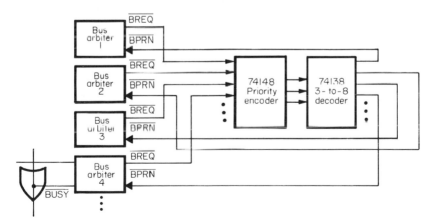

Fig. 4.9   Parallel priority resolving.

propagated to the BPRO* output. A transfer request, if no BPRN* input exists, which indicates that there is no higher priority request, causes a BPRO* output to signal all lower priority masters. The bus is captured when it is idle (busy active state).

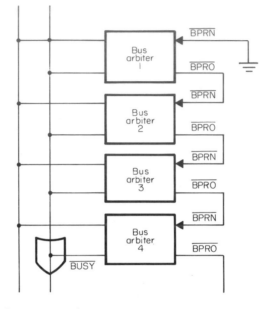

Fig. 4.10 Serial priority resolving.

An interesting feature of the bus arbiter is the implementation of semaphores by means of a locked test and set condition. The bus arbiter prevents the use of the shared bus while a microprocessor is operating on a semaphore.

Using the bus arbiter introduced above, a number of multi-microprocessor design options are possible using a shared parallel bus. The first one, called single-bus mode, allows a single bus to be shared by all microprocessors, memory, and input–output devices. There are disadvantages in using a single transfer medium for all memory accesses and input–output operations. Clearly the shared bus can quickly become a bottleneck.

The second option possible is to separate the input–output devices dedicated to a microprocessor and connect them by means of a local input–output bus, as shown in Fig. 4.11. This means that the memory and input–output space are separated. Thus input–output commands are treated locally to each microprocessor which then uses the shared bus when access to shared resources is needed.

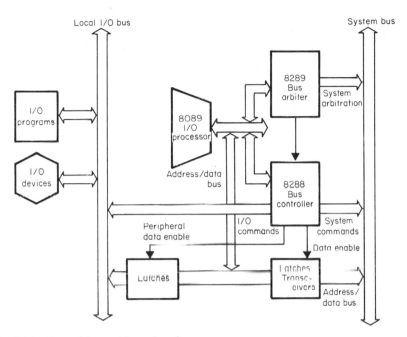

Fig. 4.11   Shared bus with no local memory.

The third option, which is the extension of the second, is to have a local bus for each microprocessor with local memory and input–output devices (see Fig. 4.12). The microprocessor normally operates through its local bus, fetching instructions, executing input–output instructions, and so on. Thus all microprocessors can function without interference so long as their bus cycles are performed on their local buses. When a system bus transfer is needed, the bus arbiter with the bus controller then implements the necessary access. Selection of the local or system bus can be made on an address mapping basis. In Fig. 4.12 both sets of addresses are shown. Microprocessors can communicate with both a resident bus and a multimaster system bus. In such a system configuration, the processor would have access to the memory and peripherals of both buses. Memory mapping techniques can be applied to select which bus to access. The system bus–resident bus input on the arbiter determines whether or not the system bus is to be accessed. It also enables or disables commands from one of the bus controllers. In such a system configuration, it is possible to issue both memory and input–output commands to either bus and, as a result, two bus controllers are needed, one for each bus.

In Fig. 4.12, memory mapping techniques are applied on the resident bus side of the system rather than on the multiprocessor or system bus. In this

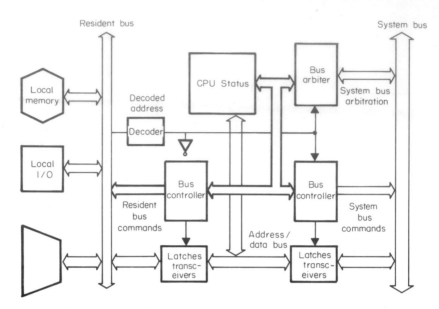

Fig. 4.12 Shared bus with local memory.

case both sets of address latches (resident bus and system bus) are latched with the same address by their respective bus controllers. The system bus address latches, however, may or may not be enabled, depending upon when the arbiter has bus access. The resident bus address latches are always enabled; hence, the memory mapping technique is applied to the resident bus.

A simpler system with an 8086 or 8088 microprocessor can exist if it is desirable to have only PROM, read only memory, or read only peripheral interfaces on the resident bus. These microprocessors additionally generate a read signal in conjunction with the bus controller signals. By using this read signal and memory mapping, microprocessors can operate from a local program store without contending for use of the system bus. This technique eliminates the need for a second bus controller.

In operation, both bus controllers respond to the processor status line and both simultaneously issue an address latch enable strobe to their respective address latches. Both bus controllers issue command and control signals unless inhibited. The purpose of the memory mapping circuits is to inhibit one of the bus controllers before contention or erroneous commands can occur.

4.3   Serial Bus Structures

Beyond a distance of ten metres or so the parallel bus ceases to be suitable for interconnecting microprocessors, due to attenuation and delays introduced by distance. In this case, serial transmission methods can be used for linking microprocessors (or clusters of microprocessors) distributed over some geographical distance. Traditionally the telephone system has been used as the data transmission medium to interconnect computer systems. Modems are required to convert the digital signals to analogue form suitable for transmission. Data rates that can normally be achieved are 110–48 000 bit/s. The expense and bulkiness of modems and their relatively low data rates make such systems unattractive for linking microprocessors. Instead, to cover shorter distances up to 1 km, several interconnection mechanisms have been emerging, named local area networks [6]. These provide inexpensive transmission media with data rates as high as 10 Mbit/s. Twisted pair and coaxial cable is most commonly used for transmission. Fibre optic cable is also very promising, with its higher bandwidth and excellent noise immunity properties. At the moment, however, it is still more costly generally and there are difficulties in attaching multiple devices.

Serial bus structures, as introduced in Chapter 3, enable local networks of microprocessors to be built. As shown in Fig. 4.13, messages are passed

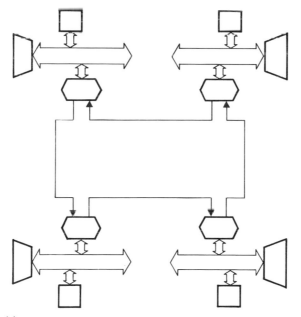

Fig. 4.13   Serial bus.

unidirectionally from node to node through a repeater until they reach their destination. A repeater usually includes demodulation buffering and remodulation of message received in a serial form. Messages, in addition to their information content, include the destination–source as well as control and error-handling information.

A Control Token Passing Ring Example

As an example, we will consider the serial data bus developed by Litton Data Systems, USA [8]. It features a 20 Mbit/s serial data transmission rate over coaxial cable or fibre optic lines. As shown in Fig. 4.14a there are two loops circulating in opposite directions, called the primary loop and the secondary loop.

This redundancy is provided so that a single node failure does not mean the shut down of the complete system. In normal operations the primary loop is used to transfer data with the secondary loop carrying a predefined idle pattern. This, in effect, enables each node to constantly monitor both loops. If there is a node failure such as shown in Fig. 4.14b, both adjacent nodes detect the loss of incoming information. Node A loses the idle pattern and node B loses the data. Hardware or software within nodes A and B will choose a path that connects the primary loop to the secondary one. This causes data to flow in both loops, keeping the bus functioning and isolating the failed node.

The data bus consists of three hardware components: the data bus node, the transmission link, and the bus interface (SIB interface) card, each of which can handle two loops, the primary and a backup. Bus interface hardware partitioning is required to: allow independent operation of the transmit/receive (T/R) assemblies as data repeaters when the SIB interface card or element has failed; provide the capability to reconfigure the bus; permit interchangeability of coaxial cable and fibre optic T/R assemblies; contain the SIB interface logic on a single card; and minimize the amount of redundant logic on the T/R assembly. Implementation of the bus interface hardware providing access to the data bus is shown in Fig. 4.14c.

The transmission format which is similar to IBM's synchronous data link control (SDLC) is shown in Table 4.I. The transmission starts with a go-ahead pattern which consists of a zero followed by consecutive ones that is issued by the current bus controller, and this indicates that the bus is available for transmission. Each node then samples for the go-ahead pattern to determine the bus availability. When a node has a message for transmission it converts the go-ahead pattern to a flag (zero followed by five ones followed by zero). Therefore, each message has the 8-bit start flag, and one 8-bit closing flag. In order to prevent these combinations appearing within the message itself, the insertion of zeros at the transmitter and

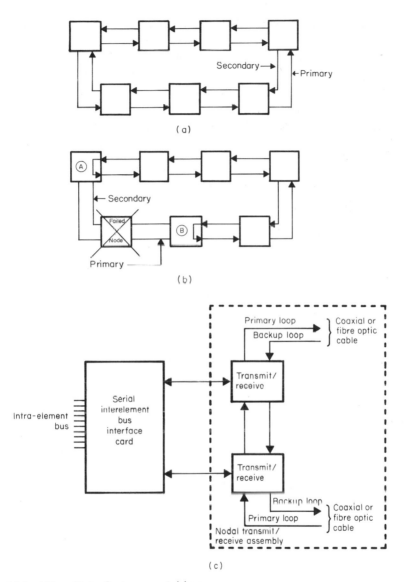

Fig. 111   Litton Data Systems serial bus.

deletion of them at the receiver are features similar to SDLC. In the table
the first 8-bit denotes the destination, which is followed by a 6-bit control
part followed by an 8-bit source address. There are four destination address
categories:

   1. global: all nodes will accept the message (broadcast);

2. device collective: all nodes of a given type (such as terminals) will accept the message. There are six types of devices;
3. unique: only the addressed node will accept the message;
4. bus controller: only the active controller will accept the message.

The control field is used for acknowledgement of received messages, requests to send, permission to send, and several system control messages. A 16-bit field message length defines the word count of the message which includes all words (16-bit) between the beginning and ending flags. A checksum follows the data and precedes the closing flag.

Table 4.1   SIB transmission format.

Go-ahead (Flag)[a]	Flag(F_O)	A_T	C_1	C_2	A_F	ML	Information	EC	Flag(F_E)

	Field	Length	Comments
	Go-ahead (flag)	8 bits	0 1 1 1 1 1 1 1
F_O	Opening flag	8 bits	0 1 1 1 1 1 1 0
A_T	Destination address	8 bits	Address table
C_1	System control	8 bits	Control table
C_2	User control	8 bits	System software
A_F	Source address	8 bits	See Address table
ML	Message length	16 bits	Number of words in message
I	Information	0 to 4092 words	No format restrictions on software
EC	Error check	16 bits	Module $2^{16} - 1$ sum of all words after F_O
F_E	Ending flag	8 bits	0 1 1 1 1 1 1 0

[a]Converted to flag pattern by SIB Interface card.

A bus controller is assigned responsibility for establishing bus operations and resetting all nodes during start-up. The bus controller also periodically checks the status of all nodes on the bus. A major function of the bus controller is to provide check synchronization for the loop, issue the initial go-ahead pattern (token), and ensure that initial go-ahead is always present in the loop.

Message transmission is achieved without intervention of the system bus controller. All messages sent by any node to any other node(s) are addressed directly and proceed directly to the addressees, and acknowledgments are sent directly to the addressors. As each node sees the go-ahead pattern go by, it has the opportunity to insert its message on the bus. When it does, it changes the go-ahead pattern to an opening flag, signalling the start of its message. At the end of its transmission, the node appends the closing flag and a go-ahead pattern to allow other nodes in the loop to transmit. Access to the bus is guaranteed to all nodes as each message proceeds around the bus. No node has the bus for transmission of more than one message at a time, and the go-ahead pattern is constantly and automatically moving from one node to the next. There is not time lost for nodes that have no messages to place on the bus, as occurs in a time division multiplex system.

As messages move around the loop, each node looks for its unique group or global address to determine whether or not the message is for this node. The bus controller node also looks for the dedicated bus controller address. If the message is for the node, it is stored in memory at the node and a processor within the node is informed. In any event, the message continues around the loop until it is returned to the sending node, where it is stripped from the bus. Nodes in the loop, therefore, act as repeaters rather than as store and forward nodes.

4.4   Contention Bus Structures

Contention bus principles were introduced in the previous chapter. Here an outline of a specific example, namely the Ethernet, is presented. This was first developed by Xerox Corporation as a means to build local area networks. The word "ether" refers to the medium where electromagnetic waves were believed to propagate in space. The Aloha net mentioned earlier used, in fact, radio waves for communication. Ethernet uses a coaxial cable in which we can imagine that the "ether" has been encapsulated. The stations that are connected contend for the common broadcast communications channel contained in the coaxial cable. Existing cable TV technology has been used for the actual cable. Stations are connected to the cable using standard cable taps which pierce the coaxial shield and the core dielectric and contact the centre conductor. The tap is then connected to a transceiver, as shown in Fig. 4.15. Coaxial cable is terminated at each end. The cable can then be laid in a building and taps taken as required. The maximum length of the cable is about 1 km, with transmission speeds reaching 10 Mbit/s.

The functions of a transceiver are shown in Fig. 4.15 [9] It contains a small quantity of electronics to drive and receive signals on the cable, detect collisions, maintain ground isolation, and protect the cable from certain failures of the transceiver, controller, or host. Data on the cable is Manchester encoded, thus bits are phase-encoded in the controller before being passed on to the transceiver. The coding scheme used implies that there is always a transition in the middle of the bit cell: a positive edge corresponds to a "one" and a negative edge to a "zero" bit (Fig. 4.16a). The carrier is detected by the presence of transmission on the cable. When no transmitter is active, the channel is quiescent in the "off" state.

Collision is detected by comparing the received data with that being transmitted, and producing a collision signal whenever there is a difference. Using Manchester coding, the transmitter is off for half of each bit period,

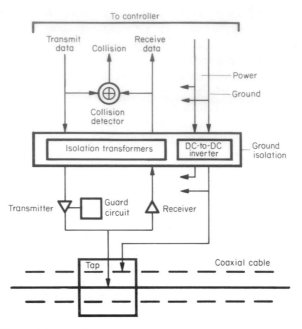

Fig. 4.15   Ethernet transceiver.

as illustrated in Fig. 4.16a. Thus, if there are simultaneous transmissions during the off periods of a transmitter, the other station's signal is detected indicating a collision. This is implemented by an Exclusive-OR circuit, as shown in Fig. 4.15.

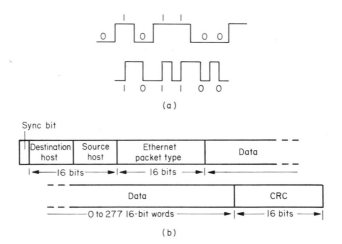

Fig. 4.16   Ethernet packet format. (a) Manchester encoding. (b) Packet format.

The controller is the circuit used between the transceiver and the host machine. Phase-encoder and phase-decoder circuits implement the Manchester encoding and decoding respectively, and produce serial bit streams. The Ethernet packet format that is handled is shown in Fig. 4.16b. The Synch bit indicates the beginning of a packet. Destination and source addresses are 8-bits each. The next 18 bits are used to indicate the packet type used by the next level communication protocol. The data transmitted could be of variable length, from 0 to 277 16-bit words. The last 16-bits are treated as a cyclic redundancy code (CRC) used for error detecting. This is done by the CRC circuit shown in Fig. 4.17. A FIFO queue is used as a buffer stage for received packets and packets that are being prepared for transmission. The address detection is done while bits are received at the shift register. The scheme shown here is half-duplex, where the controller shares circuits for both receipt and transmission of packets. By using additional hardware a full-duplex controller can be designed. Clearly, many design options exist here so that the speed of processor and control circuits can be well matched to the speed of the Ethernet transmission.

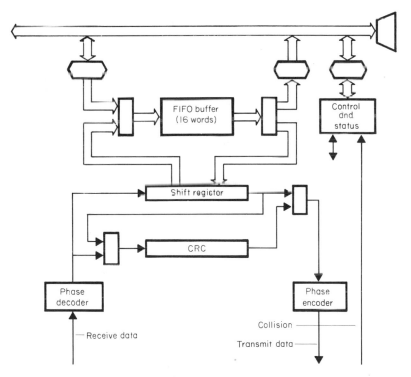

Fig. 4.17   Ethernet controller hardware.

A collision occurs when a transmitter fails to defer to another transmission already in progress. Before transmission the absence of the carrier is ensured. When a collision is detected, the controller ceases data transmission immediately and turns the transmitter on for three microseconds before shutting down. This signal ensures that all participants in the collision are made aware of it and they also in turn shut down. Following a collision a timer is started, set to a random value computed using a "binary exponential back-off algorithm". This sets the mean value of the interval as twice that of the previous interval. The delay following a collision is uniformly distributed between 0 to $(2^n - 1)$, where n is the number of previous unsuccessful attempts to transmit the packet. Hardware could be built to produce the necessary random delays. The actual delay time chosen is the product of the random number with the maximum contention interval or "slot" time. This is the maximum time between starting a transmission and detecting a collision, one end-to-end round-trip delay (about forty microseconds).

4.5   Point-to-point Communication

The parallel bus, serial bus, and contention bus schemes discussed above have a common characteristic in that each microprocessor connected to the bus listens continuously to the messages on the bus to see whether there is one addressed to it. Since the bus is a shared medium, the access to it for a sender needs arbitration.

In point-to-point communication networks a private line is allocated between a sender and receiver microprocessor. Since the microprocessors in general interchange the roles of sender and receiver, the private line then is either duplex, semiduplex or a separate line dedicated to each direction of transfer.

A variety of systems developed for the data communications field can be used to establish the point-to-point links. These could implement a serial or parallel transmission scheme. A serial scheme could consist of asynchronous character-by-character transmission, or synchronous transmission to achieve higher speeds. A parallel scheme can be achieved by transferring one byte at a time where each bit is transmitted by a separate line. In all these methods a simple handshake mechanism is needed to implement the data transfer.

When interconnecting microprocessors by means of point-to-point lines a topology emerges, as illustrated in Fig. 4.18. In this structure only the neighbouring nodes are assumed to communicate. If the requirements are such that all nodes need to communicate with all the other nodes then a communication line needs to be allocated between all pairs of microprocessors. For an N node network this necessitates $N(N-1)/2$ lines. As shown in Table 4.II this number grows with the square of N. The number of lines that each processor has to handle, $M = N-1$, is a linear function of N. Clearly the number of lines grows very quickly so that beyond about four node multi-microprocessors this approach becomes impracticable.

Table 4.II

N	$N(N-1)/2$	$M = N-1$
4	12	3
8	56	7
16	240	15
32	992	31
64	4 032	63
128	16 265	127
256	65 280	265

The alternative is to adopt the methods developed for computer communication networks. In the store and forward networks, intermediate nodes are used to provide communication between nodes with no immediate connection. For this purpose routing techniques are used.

A routing mechanism is the collection of procedures used to control node-to node information flow in computer communication networks. A routing mechanism, in addition to ensuring the integrity of transmitted information, has to ensure the optimum use of resources, such as finding the shortest route between a sender and receiver, avoiding congestion, and so on.

Extensive literature exists for routing aspects related to computer communication networks [10]. Here a summary of the main approaches used will be presented. The routing approach to be adopted depends on many features and relates closely to the main architectural approach. For example, whether the control strategy is centralized or distributed affects the routing methods to be used. The information about the system's topology, whether it is local (centralized) or global (distributed) also affects the routing strategy. Finally the approach could be deterministic or random (stochastic).

Saturation routing

A message received by a node, if it is not destined for that node, is transmitted to all neighbours except the one from which the message was received. If the same message is received for the second time it is not retransmitted. This ensures that unwanted messages eventually will be removed from the system and the process eventually terminates. Clearly saturation routing works for smaller systems with low message traffic. It is, however, simpler to implement, and the technique is not dependent on the system topology. Therefore link or node failures are not catastrophic for the transmission mechanism to continue to function. (That is until the network splits into disjoint subnets; the system continues to function still within each subnet.)

Random routing

Messages are routed according to a random selection of links. A message arriving at an intermediate node is routed to the link selected according to some probability distribution. Random routing is also simple to implement and does not require the topology information. It is, however, inefficient since a message may have to traverse a large number of nodes before it finds its destination.

Fixed routing

Fixed routing is the classic mechanism which relies on a routing matrix derived for a given topology. For example, in Fig. 4.18b the routing matrix

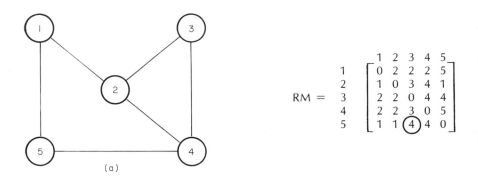

Fig. 4.18   Fixed routing. (a) Network. (b) Routing table.

is given which corresponds to the network topology of Fig. 4.18a. Thus, for example, a message at node 5 destined for node 3 is sent to node 4 (circled). This message at node 4 is sent to node 3 which is adjacent. Thus for each node in a routing matrix there corresponds a row. Each node then needs to store the corresponding routing matrix in order to select the proper adjacent node once a message is received.

The routing tables are generated so as to satisfy certain performance characteristics, e.g. that messages follow shortest paths [11]. Once a routing table is generated it can either be kept in a routing control centre, which then distributes the appropriate information to the nodes, or the whole routing information is distributed without recourse to a central point. Any change of routing conditions such as a failure requires updating the routing tables at the nodes.

Adaptive techniques

The fixed routing technique explained above functions on paths established *a priori*, regardless of the prevailing traffic conditions. Again, relying on a global or local mechanism, routing can be adjusted to take into account the existing traffic conditions. The criteria normally used is to minimize end-to-end message delay time (as distinct from minimum path length). One way of doing this is to maintain a delay table where each entry indicates the time needed from a given node to go to the destination node via one of the possible neighbours. Clearly then the route to choose means finding the minimum time entry neighbour at each node. The method involves each node periodically to send a minimum delay sector to all of its neighbours to modify delay tables [12].

Adaptive routing techniques are relatively complex and they require more processing and storage overheads as compared to previous techniques. On the other hand, they are more adaptable to varying traffic conditions. They have been used successfully in heterogenous computer communication networks.

References

[1] Intel Multibus Specification, Intel Corporation, 1978.
[2] Z. Bender. ZBI: a system bus for the Z8000, *Mini-Micro Systems*, June 1980, pp. 67–75.
[3] K. A. Elmquist, M. Fullmer, B. B. Gustavson and G. Morrow. Standard specification for S-100 bus interface devices, *IEEE Computer*, July 1979, pp. 28–52.
[4] Proposed Microcomputer System 796 bus standard, *IEEE Computer*, October 1980, pp. 89–105.
[5] J. Nadim and B. McCormich. Bus arbiter streamline multimicroprocessor design, *Computer Design*, June 1980.
[6] J. M. Kryskow and C. K. Miller. Local area networks overview—part 1: definitions and attributes, *Computer Design,* February 1981, pp. 19–35.
[7] B. D. Clarke, K. T. Program and B. P. Read. An introduction to local area

networks, *Proceedings of the IEEE*, November 1978, pp. 1497–1517.

[8] R. Maurello. A distributed processing system for military applications—part 2: the serial data bus, *Computer Design*, October 1980, pp. 14–36.

[9] C. R. Crane and E. A. Taft. Practical considerations in Ethernet local network design, *Hawaii International Conference on System Sciences*, January 1980.

[10] D. W. Davies,   D. L. Barber,   W. L. Price   and   C. M. Solomonides. "Computer Networks and their Protocols", John Wiley and Sons, Chichester, UK, 1979.

[11] M. Bozygit and Y. Paker. A fixed routing problem in large and high correctivity networks, *BCS The Computer Journal*, **22**, No. 3, 1979.

[12] G. L. Fultz.   Adaptive   routing   techniques   for   message   computer communication, Ph.D. thesis, USCLA, June 1972.

Chapter 5

System Design Fundamentals

5.1 Introduction

With the increased interest in multi-microprocessor and distributed computing systems, there is emerging a large number of proposals and approaches to handle them. Yet there are very few system design tools at our disposal which have been fully developed and universally accepted to make the building of these machines a straightforward engineering process. Many methods proposed are at the experimental and research stage, and many machines built are more characteristic of prototypes than products. The great variety of application areas and requirements, and architectural options makes it difficult to arrive at a common denominator of practice. Consequently, the current approach relies on the methods developed for mono-processors and their extensions such as multi-programming and point-to-point communication. Most systems, then, are constructed in an *ad hoc* manner to meet the specifications of a given environment with essentially known techniques and components [1]. In this chapter, some of the underlying issues are discussed.

The motivation for building a multi microprocessor system is different in different application environments, affecting design decisions and the factors to be considered. For example, a multi-microprocessor can be dedicated to a given application or can be shared by a number of applications. Either performance or reliability can become the dominant design factor. In each case different aspects of the overall approach become prominent.

In a multi-microprocessor design the architectural philosophy requires the interrelated consideration of application requirements, hardware, communication, and software aspects. While more detailed treatment of software issues is left until Chapter 6, each of the considerations discussed below should be seen as having implications as to the structure, hardware, and software of a system.

Most multi-microprocessors differentiate between a processor (or processing element) which is a conventional hardware unit capable of executing programs, and a process, which is a piece of software, relatively independent, capable of performing a well-defined function. The processors and their linkage reflect the underlying hardware architecture, whereas the processes and their communication reflect the software structure. Although it is generally desirable that the hardware and software structure are mirror images, this is not always true. Thus the main requirements of an application, its decomposition so as to determine an underlying structure, the design of hardware and software to match each other and eventually the application, all form part of the design process.

5.2   Types of Communication

The communication infrastructure used to construct a multi-microprocessor is perhaps one of the most important features influencing all subsequent design decisions. Here it is worth considering some of the main aspects of communication.

It is well known that, in general, communication between two processes can be either direct or indirect. In the case of direct communication either the entity that is sending and the recipient entity are both implied, such as two processes communicating over a fixed wire (Fig. 5.1a), or an identification is attached to the message to specify the sender and/or receiver (Fig. 5.1b). In the latter case, if there is receiver identification, it is the function of the transport system to locate the correct receiver among the possible receivers. Alternatively, this function can be delegated to the

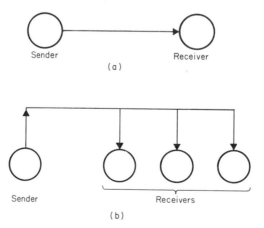

Fig. 5.1   Direct communication.

receiver stage and each receiver checks the message to ensure that it matches its own identification, in which case the message is accepted. Otherwise, the message is rejected (ignored). The identity of the sender is necessary if the recipient entity is likely to receive messages from a number of possible senders.

Clearly, this is a rather rigid system where each process has to have precise knowledge of the other processes with which it needs to correspond. This "knowledge" has to be consistent, i.e. if process A is to send messages to process B, then process A must know of the existence and the exact location of process B as a receiver, and process B must know also of the existence and the exact location of process A as a sender. For large systems it is not hard to imagine the practical difficulties involved in maintaining overall consistency. In practice, one approach is to allow all address

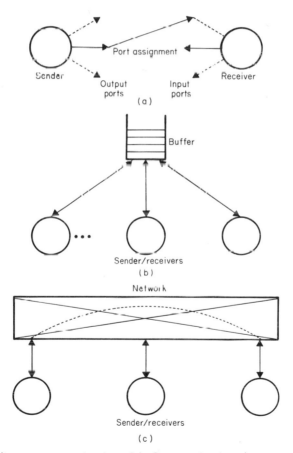

Fig. 5.2   Indirect communication. (a) Communication by ports. (b) Mailbox communication. (c) Network communication.

combinations, and not to check consistency. In case of changes, such as replacing one process by another, or changing the site of a process, alterations are needed in all processes which refer to the process changed.

Indirect communication involves an intermediate stage between processes where destination addresses are managed. Some systems achieve this by the mechanism of ports [2]. Each process communicates via ports allocated to that process. Output ports are linked externally to input ports, as illustrated in Fig. 5.2a. The process is then concerned with what port to use without any knowledge of what other process it will be linked to during the run time. Appropriate linkage is the job of the intermediate stage. In another approach, named buffer channels are the intermediate entities for communication. They are independent but can be allocated to a process. The mailbox scheme is an example (Fig. 5.2b) where a number of processes share a common buffer. The indirect communication medium could take the form of a network (Fig. 5.2c) where a transport protocol ensures point-to-point message transmission. This is explained below by means of a particular implementation [3].

Figure 5.3 illustrates a store–forward communication scheme as utilized in VTM using an indirect communication scheme based on computers interconnected by means of a physical network. Processes which exist at node computers refer to other processes by means of logical names (addresses). The routing establishes the link between the processes. Thus the matching of logical names to physical location is implicit in the routing mechanism, hence in each routing table that is maintained at communication computers. Store–forward communication requires buffers at node computer shared by local processes and at communication computers to

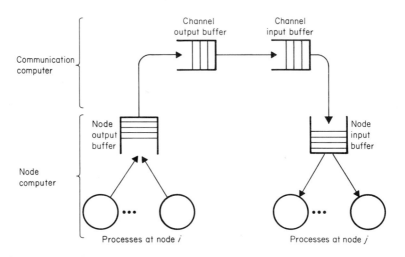

Fig. 5.3   Variable topology multicomputer store-forward communication.

handle routing, as illustrated in Fig. 5.3. Known synchronization mechanisms are used so that several processes can share a single buffer. Note that when the channel buffer (Fig. 5.3) is full there is a likelihood of the system clogging. Therefore, the store–forward communication schemes also incorporate some flow-control mechanism to adjust the traffic distribution to avoid congestion.

5.3 Process Co-ordination and Priority

A distributed computer system consists of a number of co-operating processes which interact in some prescribed manner. This interaction manifests itself essentially in the following ways.

1. One process initiating (triggering) another one. This requires the intervention of the underlying control mechanism.
2. Two processes communicating with each other.
3. One process inquiring about the state of the other.

Any process in the system goes through several phases. The initial phase involves the activation procedures which happen when a process is introduced to the system. The second phase may be called the "cognizance" stage, when each process ensures the existence of other processes with which it needs to interact during its execution. The third phase is the execution of the process. The fourth and final phase is termination, when a process is removed from the system.

When a process is introduced the system must take note of this so that appropriate mechanisms, such as routing, are updated.

Cognizance involves a process making sure that the processes with which it needs to interact do exist in the system, and they are activated [3]. One mechanism to do this would be an ACTIVATE NAMELIST command. This command has the control effect of starting the execution of other processes. If a process in the NAMELIST is not known to the system then the calling process cannot proceed. The response of a process which is initiated by an ACTIVATE command could be a status message indicating that the process is located and has started execution.

This type of "free for all" activate mechanism may not be desirable for large systems with large numbers of processes. In particular, the deadlock problem may become uncontrollable. For example, to introduce constraints for the activate mechanism it is possible for VTM to authorize ACTIVATE command only for those processes connected through predetermined virtual links.

Cognizance is also related to process allocation if multiple copies of a process exist at a given node or at several nodes. A network through virtual link mechanism is then required to allocate one of the multiple processes to the calling process. This link is maintained throughout the life of the interaction.

Clearly, another approach is to separate the activate and cognizance phases. Process activation may be seen as a control function vested to a distributed operating system and the cognizance function can be left to the individual processes. A special instruction is needed to simply check the states of the interacting processes and block further execution if any one of them is not activated. More detailed discussion of these issues is left to Chapter 6.

Efficient scheduling is a major concern in parallel systems. To help in this, and in handling contention for the shared resources, some sort of priority scheme needs to be introduced in distributed systems. Priority structures could either be static (hardware) or dynamically variable (programmable). In the static case, priorities for message communication statements would be assigned at the time of the process creation/definition based on the types of messages involved. In the dynamic case, the priorities could be made to be a function of various types of information which varies in time.

The notion of priorities being associated with message communication statements makes sense only if non-deterministic message communication constructs are permitted. This is the case when message communication statements are allowed to appear in the guards of guarded commands: i.e. when multiple message communication statements within a process are eligible for execution and only one of them can be executed, then the choice of which one to execute would be determined by the associated priorities. Language outlines like CSP assume that the underlying kernel would make sure that fair scheduling of input operations (message reception statements) in guarded commands would be done to prevent starvation.

For example, in VTM both static and semi-dynamic priority schemes exist for different reasons [3]. The packet-switched messages are assumed to be of the same priority, occupying the highest level in the priority scale. This is self-evident since these messages are used for control purposes. Data communication which is done over virtual paths can be set to different priority levels when a link is initiated. In VTM non-deterministic message communication constructs are not accepted. Yet a RECEIVE statement can have more than one input. In this case it is good practice to allocate the same priority to all of the incoming paths to avoid starvation.

5.4   Process — Processor allocation

The allocation of a process to a processor could be fixed or dynamically changed. There are clearly many advantages in fixed mapping which simplifies the management of communication between processes. However, this does not enable advantage to be taken of the potential that a multicomputer offers in terms of redundancy, sharing of resources, and handling of failures.

Dynamic mapping, on the other hand, requires the ability to move a process from one processor to another, and, therefore, a fast communication medium. One way of dealing with this problem is to maintain multiple copies of processes so that when a process is needed the one on a free processor is activated. Dynamic mapping also requires more sophisticated indirect communications.

The process–processor mapping issue also relates to bootstrapping problems as well as secondary memory management. For example, if a single mass memory device is used for bootstrapping and storing copies of processes, when the power is turned on the bootstrap process initializes each processor. Then from a control point where the mass memory is located, the processes are distributed to individual processors following a certain mapping procedure. By contrast to this centralized approach, a more distributed approach consists of providing a number of secondary storage devices, at the extreme case one per processor, to record the processes. In this case, the location of a process already implies a certain mapping condition. Thus, by fixing the position of a process at a given location, this information also needs to be acknowledged by the underlying mapping procedure so that other processes can locate the inserted process as well as the inserted process can locate the others.

Performance is an important aspect of process–processor mapping. Depending on the architecture chosen, the actual location of processes can influence performance dramatically. Since process interaction changes dynamically, the ability of process–processor mapping to follow these changes (dynamic mapping, introduced above), can also improve perform-ance. Clearly, for example, in Cm* architecture, the processes that interact frequently are placed on the same local bus. In VTM, the architectural interconnection pattern follows the process interaction.

The process–processor mapping scheme to be adopted depends to a large extent on application. If a multi-microprocessor is designed for a single well-defined application where individual processes are part of a common single program, then the architecture of the machine is much influenced by the way individual processes are identified and interact. There is a deliberate effort then in allocating processors to processes. On the other hand, in a more general-purpose application, where a multi-microprocessor is used more like a general purpose digital computer, more flexible mapping is required, making mapping an important design feature. In a transactional system, many identical operations are performed on incoming requests, and a process can then become a resource to be called upon on request. In this case, multiple copies of processes can exist on one or more processors and be allocated to specific requests. The mapping then becomes one-to-many, each time identifying and allocating a free process among many identical copies. A similar problem arises if a number of processes share a processor. The mapping scheme then needs to locate the process which resides on a free processor.

In VTM a dynamic mapping scheme is adopted where processes can be assigned to node computers as well. The interaction between the processes is established by the communication network. Each process is totally resident in a processor. If N is the size of the network and M the number of processes, when $M < N$ the system is redundant. On the other hand, if $M > N$ then some processes need to share processors.

In VTM processes are identified by names. These logical names assume a physical significance as soon as a process is assigned to a specific processor.

5.5   Network Visibility

Network visibility refers to the issue of whether or not the physical network on which the distributed program would function should be made visible at the language level. Visibility is said to exist if the language has primitives which refer to physical sites/nodes and variables of type site/node are allowed in the language. The greater the visibility, the more a user needs to take care of transport and co-ordination aspects. Less visibility means less worry about transport aspects, yet at the cost of losing control over many of the stages that intervene between two co-operating processes.

VTM adopts partial visibility where processes are assigned to physical nodes, and the locating of a specific process is seen as a network function. Yet each process invokes the network connection that is necessary to other processes. This is done by a CONNECT and DISCONNECT statement which establishes and cancels a virtual path

    TASK SOURCE
    CONNECT (PATH NAME) TO DESTINATION TASK;
    (type) INTEGER; 20 (priority)
    DISCONNECT (PATH NAME)

Note that finding the location of DESTINATION TASK is a network function. Clearly the location of a task immediately specifies its physical address. If a node computer contains more than one task, then physical address extension indicates its physical address. Thus a name is decoded as

    TASKNAME Node Computer. Extension Number

The collection of tasks at a node computer is called a task package.

The establishment of a path is a one-way device, and therefore at the recipient node it should be matched by

TASK DESTINATION
ACCEPT CONNECT (SOURCE TASK:TYPELIST)

Thus each CONNECT statement must be matched at the receiving end, by an ACCEPT CONNECT statement which in fact serves as an authorization (and checking) mechanism.

The virtual paths also have type information. This enables paths for variables of different types to be established.

5.6   Control Issues

Control issues in distributed computer systems tend to be complex since there does not appear to be an established methodology. Parallelism is a difficult concept in the world of digital computation where operations are performed sequentially, one step at a time. The control mechanisms inherent in such machines implement essentially sequential control. Many of the control mechanisms developed, such as Semaphors and Monitors, assume a uni-processor system with a kernel to handle apparent concurrency of processes, resident in the same processor as the kernel for sharing common resources (including processor and immediate access memory). Every operating system handles control and concurrency in a fashion peculiar to itself, which is not always clearly known by a user.

Some systems approach the control problem as an extension of the uni-processor control. A single processor is then entrusted to assume the control functions for the whole system. This requires that a single processor maintains consistent and up-to-date knowledge of the operation of all systems resources. It is easy to see that such a control system, although better understood and easily implemented, nevertheless is more vulnerable to faults and because it needs to communicate with the control point it is liable to create extra traffic and congestion. To alleviate the first problem, some systems allow flexibility in the choice of control site.

Another approach is to assume that no single processor has a complete picture of the system and that control is distributed. For example, in VTM there is no centralized control. Therefore every process needs to be equipped with sufficient means of control so as to carry out operations in an autonomous manner. The instruction which handles this is

ACTIVATE TASK NAMELIST

This instruction causes the start of execution of the tasks in its task name list.

To ensure that the process that is being activated can be done so only by a specified activating processes and instruction

ACCEPT ACTIVATE TASKLIST

exists. It is easy to see that the above mechanism implements the task system illustrated in Fig. 5.4. Note that if a task C is activated by task A then when task B tries to activate C this is automatically accepted. In other words, ACTIVATE ensures that a task is executed, regardless of who prompts the execution.

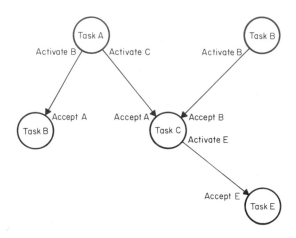

Fig. 5.4   Task system.

The instruction

STATUS TASKNAME

inquires whether a task is already running or if it is in a dormant state. Another important instruction is

TERMINATE TASKLIST

which causes a process to terminate another process. The companion instruction is

ACCEPT TERMINATE TASKLIST

a task can terminate itself by calling its own name. Another important command is

ABORT TASKLIST

with a companion instruction

ACCEPT ABORT TASKLIST

In a distributed computing system where processes are dynamically activated and de-activated, certain safeguards are needed to avoid deadlocks. For example, the system shown in Fig. 5.5a is clearly in a deadlock situation where process A expects activation from process B and vice versa. A solution in this case may be operator intervention as shown in Fig. 5.5b. To handle such situations, graphs defined by ACTIVATE-ACCEPT ACTIVATE, TERMINATE-ACCEPT TERMINATE, ABORT-ACCEPT ABORT could help. A loop indicates a possible deadlock. These graphs are also useful to check consistency (for example, every ACTIVATE has a corresponding ACCEPT-ACTIVATE).

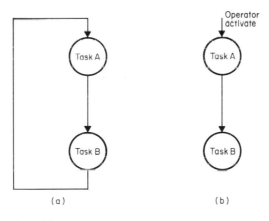

Fig. 5.5   Deadlock problem.

5.7   Synchronization

Synchronization problems are currently receiving a great deal of attention in the literature [4]. Without attempting to be comprehensive, one can distinguish several main trends:

1. Extension to existing (or proposed) sequential languages. This is the linguistic approach where the expectation is to define new constructs to handle complex distributed systems. Semaphores and Monitors are examples.
2. Study of synchronization problems by proposing certain mechanisms such as circulating tokens to handle mutual exclusion or locks (time, stamps, tickets) to handle sequencing and concurrency.

3. Distributed data base approach where the prime concern is mechanisms to ensure the consistency of data, and transactions performed on data bases distributed around different computer sites.
4. Communications approach where point-to-point data transfer and protocols ensure this is seen as the basic problem to be handled.

The difficulty is the close relationships between the basic problems: concentrating on one aspect may put out of focus the closely related issues, e.g. no token method can work unless there is a proper communication infra-structure to transport that token.

Synchronization implies that there are means of sequencing events. For example, process activation can be done with respect to a central clock, i.e. common time reference (Fig. 5.6). The central clock approach has drawbacks for implementing geographically distributed systems, when the time delays inherent in the ACTIVATE instruction could be considerable. If each node computer is allocated its own clock, the synchronizaion of these clocks poses certain fundamental problems (Fig. 5.7) [5].

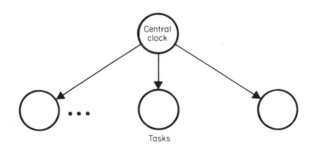

Fig. 5.6   Synchronization by central clock.

A different approach is the method called the circulating token, where each process is assumed to be on a logical ring where a unique token is passed from one process to its neighbour (Fig. 5.8). The owner of a token has certain privileges, in mutual exclusion, by virtue of being the only one having the token. The difficulty of this method is in maintaining a unique token in the system in the presence of system changes and failures [6]. As the system grows, the turn around time of a token could become considerable, introducing unduly large delays.

The meaning of synchronization differs for centralized and distributed systems. Traditionally, for monoprocessor systems, the synchronization mechanism means that of a shared resource, like a buffer, is managed by several concurrent processes which demand access to the shared resource at undetermined instances of time. In distributed computing systems, concurrent processes, in principle, reside in distinct processors and do not have direct access to a common resource, like memory, as in mono-processor systems. Rather a process provides a service to another process while the service request is in terms of a message and the response is also a message.

In a distributed computing system, where there exist complex inter-relationships between processes which change dynamically in time, a synchronization mechanism must provide means of concurrency (a number of processes initiated at the same time), mutual exclusion (when one process is activated then others must be in the de-activated state), and time sequence (a process starts only at the termination of one or more processes). The underlying mechanism should make it possible for a condition at one point of the system to be recognized by all the others so that for certain important events, a "total awareness" exists [7].

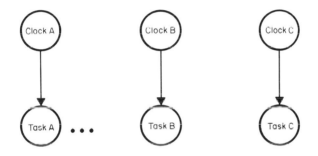

Fig. 5.7   Synchronization by distributed clocks.

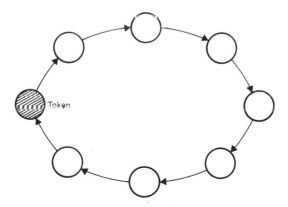

Fig. 5.8   Synchronization by circulating token.

References

[1] C. Mohan and A. Silberchatz. A perspective of distributed computing: languages, issues and applications, in "Advances in Distributed Processing Management", Vol. II, Heyden, London, 1981.

[2] A. Silberschatz. Port directed communication, *The Computer Journal*, **24**, No. 1, February 1981.

[3] Y. Paker. Virtual path management in variable topology multicomputer systems, European Research Office, US Army, (Grant No. DAERO-77-6-000), November 1977.

[4] C. A. R. Hoare. Synchronization of parallel processes, in "Book and Advanced Techniques for Microprocessor Systems", F. K. Hanna, ed., Peter Perigrinus, London, 1980, pp. 108–111.

[5] L. Lamport. The synchronization of independent processes, *Akta Informations*, **7**, Fasc. 1, 1976.

[6] G. Le Lann. Distributed systems—towards a formal approach, *IFIP Congress 77*, Toronto, August 77, pp. 155–160.

[7] Y. Paker. Control, synchronization and reconfigurability problems, in "Variable Topology Multicomputer Systems", European Research Office, US Army, (Grant No. DA-ERO-78-G-110), October 1980.

Chapter 6

Software

6.1 General Considerations

In an environment of declining hardware costs, the relative importance of software is growing, often making it the major cost item, particularly if only one or a few copies of an application is to be produced. Yet, at the moment, there is a dearth of software methodology able to cope with the requirements of multi-microprocessor systems. There has been much research work and interest in various aspects of distributed and parallel computing software, yet relatively few principles and tools have emerged which are generally accepted and applied by the majority of systems designers. The fundamental reason for this state of affairs is the conceptual difference between mono- and multi-processor systems, designed for dealing with sequential and parallel operations respectively. Most software methodologies have been developed for mono-processors. Thus the initial multi-processor systems attempted to use the software tools already available and adapt them to the new conditions. This, of course, did not always work. In particular, full parallelism offered by the multi-processor systems could not be fully exploited. Software, then, is still the main stumbling block in the widespread use of multi-microprocessors.

On a more practical level, the continuing development of micro-processors over the last decade has meant a constant evolution of software tools available for microprocessors. Initially, with 8-bit microprocessors, only elementary software development tools were available, namely assemblers. Since microcomputer systems initially lacked adequate hardware and software support in terms of secondary memory and software development tools, most program writing took place on mainframe machines with cross-assemblers. The early microprocessors also did not have adequate architectural features to support the higher level languages and operating systems. With improvements in technology, and especially with 16-bit machines, however, things changed dramatically. These machines now contain high level language compilers and operating systems. The architectures of modern microprocessors take into account the support features for language translators and operating systems such as context switching. In fact, one recent microprocessor, Intel 432, has been developed to support a particular high level language, Ada [1]. Today, for software development, microcomputer configurations are sufficiently large to make such systems self sufficient. Therefore, the emphasis has been shifting more and more to use the target machine for software development. The underlying tendency in microprocessor software development, like the minicomputer case that preceded it [2], has been to adopt and adapt the software concepts developed for large machines; e.g. in the use first of Basic as the high level interactive language and then in the introduction of Fortran and Cobol as larger size memories became available. The use of more recent languages such as Pascal has been slower. Clearly, the availability of common languages across the micro–mini–mainframe range provided a mechanism for channelling the experiences acquired with larger machines to smaller ones. Yet, at the same time, this somewhat hindered the development of fresh new ideas based on the micros.

Any software written explicitly or implicitly makes use of the underlying hardware structure. For example, in a high level language, if we write

$$A = B * C$$

it is implicit that the entities that we refer to as A, B, and C are all in the immediate access memory. It is also implicit that this memory is randomly accessible and no searching is needed. Access to a file, on the other hand, implies that the entities we are searching are on a disc with serial access capabilities. Various sequences of operations that need to be carried out to access a data item, say on a disc, have been made transparent to the user. This, however, does not detract from the fact that a language construct such as

READ   1   X,Y

refers to a file located on a disc medium. A programmer then has to take this into account while coding an application. The reason why there are high level language standards which are, to a varying degree, universally accepted is because there is a standard digital computer architecture which is based on a single central processor operating on a main memory coupled to a hierarchy of secondary memories.

Unfortunately, this universally understood architecture no longer applies in the case of multi-microprocessor systems. As explained in the preceding chapter, there are great variations in the multi-microprocessor architectures. There are also various reasons for building a multi-microprocessor. It could be required for a dedicated real-time process control where an application might be composed of well-defined, autonomous but interacting tasks, or it could be needed to solve parallel structured algorithms. A multi-microprocessor system could be constructed for transaction processing or as a general purpose computer with improved performance. Fault-tolerance could be the main purpose in providing a multiplicity of hardware and software for building highly reliable computers. The distributed software methodology that is required should be able to provide the underlying systems software for implementing vastly varying systems for widely different purposes, as well as adequate software production and testing tools to write application software. Since distributed systems undergo significant changes during their life cycle, software needs to be modular to incorporate these changes.

The question of whether or not the target machine can also be used for program development is an open one. Clearly in loosely coupled machines where processor nodes are geographically distributed, the program modules that constitute an application need to be developed, tested, and debugged on a host machine (preferably of the same type as the target machine). Tools are therefore needed to create an environment as close to the real environment as possible to test the interaction of separate modules.

Much work that has been done in structured programming to separate a mono-processor program into well-defined modules, and attempts to systematize the interactions between modules, have helped to achieve a more disciplined approach to software development with much benefit to multi-microprocessor software. However, many of these ideas and implementations rely on the underlying architecture of mono-processors. A more drastic departure from the conventional concepts are needed to deal with the growing numbers of distributed computers. It is comforting to see that distributed computers take the ideas of modularization and autonomous process interaction a step further; this forces a certain programming discipline. Local networks are already introducing an architectural uniformity and size required for the widespread use of such systems.

In multi-microprocessor systems the architectural structure, application requirements, and varied software aspects like the operating system, communication infrastructure, and tools to aid application programming such as high level languages suitable for parallel programming, all form a tightly knit situation in which it is far more difficult to isolate the constituent parts and arrive at universally accepted solutions.

This chapter presents various issues relevant to operating systems development, communications, and language aspects of multi-microprocessor systems. The objective is to present a discussion of issues and some of the current approaches rather than a well-developed methodology of software, which has yet to be developed.

6.2   Distributed Operating Systems

Operating Systems

An operating system is an essential program that resides in a computer and acts as an interface between the user or an application program and the base machine [3]. An operating system, then, hides the intricate details of hardware from a user and makes it possible to utilize simple commands. It also provides a means of management of hardware and software resources such as input–output and file management [4].

The first computers did not have an operating system. This is also true of early microprocessors and most of the current embedded microcomputers. Thus these machines had to be operated by machine language instructions exercising the raw machine operations. As computers became more complex, it became clear that some of the routine operations, such as initialization (bringing the machine to a well-known state) and initial program loading (bootstrapping), had to be automated. To make a computer easier to use the complexities of the base machine had to be hidden from the user. The management of input–output, for example, became an important operating system function. With the increasing complexity and size of computers, operating systems assumed more and more functions to the extent that in large mainframe machines the base machine facilities are no longer available to the user and all machine capabilities are accessed under the operating system. Therefore, the complexities of the operating systems also have grown.

The first such systems were designed for single job handling. Then came batch processing as an outcome of improvements in secondary memory devices. Multi-programming concepts followed, improving throughput and efficiency by keeping the input–output devices and processor busy as much as possible. Time-sharing operating systems were designed to enable a number of users to have simultaneous access to a single powerful computing resource. Real-time operating systems were developed, on the one hand, for dealing with transaction processing systems, and, on the other hand, for dealing with time critical, on-line operations, particularly for process control.

For a computer manufacturer, an operating system is essential software that must be produced alongside a new machine range. Development and maintenance costs have been high, sometimes affecting crucially the success of a given computer range. An operating system also represents an important overhead where before a machine can do useful work a certain amount of memory, both primary and secondary, has to be allocated. During the run time, when an operating system facility is required, some time is spent in execution which slows down the overall operation. This is a price that needs to be paid against the greatly improved over-all performance of general-purpose computers. Protection is also an important aspect, individual users being isolated so that they cannot perform operations inadvertently affecting others. Program synchronization techniques ensure that no unwanted interaction exists when a single resource is shared.

Characteristics of Multi-microprocessor Systems

As in the case of the mono-processor, the successful design and implementation of a multi-microprocessor system relies on a well conceived operating system. There is a fundamental difference in the approach to be taken in designing the operating system. If the mono-processor operating system concepts are applied to multi-microprocessor systems indiscriminately it often leads to difficulties owing to the basic architectural differences. A single computer operating system is centralized so the state of the whole system can be monitored and the total resources of the system are available to the operating system. With a multi-microprocessor system we have tightly or loosely coupled elements, interconnected with communication means, each element having a restricted environment and partial knowledge of the state of the elements and resources. This clearly influences the approach to be taken in designing operating systems [5].

In centralized systems one observes that a certain amount of concurrency exists, e.g. independent input–output processors. Multi-programming, time-sharing, and real-time systems incorporate concurrent processes. Yet the synchronization and communication tools for such systems rely on centrally shared objects such as semaphores, monitors, mailbox, etc. Although processes are concurrent, the centralized computer provides quasi or apparent parallelism; in other words, while at a given instant only one process is executed the system behaves as if all the processes are being executed at the same time. In one way it is significant in that there is no advantage to be gained in the parallel structuring of an application since eventually the problem is solved sequentially.

Distributed systems inherently run parallel processes. Therefore it is essential that a proper framework exists for concurrent processes to communicate and co-operate in order to achieve a given application objective. The operating system functions ranging from simple initialization, bootstrapping, to more complex aspects such as resource allocation, maintenance of data consistency, fault detection and recovery, etc. all have to be implemented with the above premise in mind.

Modularity has been quoted as one of the main advantages of multi-microprocessor systems. Hardware structure makes it possible to add more modules as the processing load increases, or application requirements change. To deal with faults, one processor can be interchanged with another. Multi-processing gives us a means of sharing the load among the individual processors. The underlying operating system, however, must be capable of handling structural changes in a system due to unexpected events like a fault, or deliberate modifications like adding another module to meet changing requirements.

An important aspect of a multi-microprocessor system is the underlying communication subsystem. In centralized systems, communication is provided by the main memory, usually implicitly. An underlying communication structure is essential for application processes to interact as well as for distributed operating system implementation. Communication aspects will be discussed later in more detail.

In centralized systems security is needed to prevent unauthorized accesses to protected data. This is achieved by means of various checks either in the application program or in the operating system itself. These methods mainly rely on centralization of information such as passwords, access control lists, etc. To help with security, hardware mechanisms, such as memory management with access rights, could be provided. For tightly coupled multi-microprocessor systems like Cm*, where the memory space is accessible for all processors, a sophisticated system of capabilities is used [6]. A capability identifies a memory area referred to by a name, and records a set of rights indicating which of the defined accesses are permitted to be performed in that memory area.

In a distributed system, data in one site is normally accessed by a process in another site by means of messages. Thus in addition to the error-free transport of data by the communication subsystem, data security by message access needs to be ensured. The nature of the distributed system, however, enhances a certain discipline of data access and transport by communication. Sometimes this can be overlooked easily in centralized systems.

Since the multi-microprocessor systems are inherently modular, it is thus natural that the software system also has a modular structure. In certain applications such modularity is self evident. In a loosely coupled structure, for example, if each processor is dedicated to perform a specific task then there is one-to-one correspondence between the application hardware–software modularity in that a given job at a given location is performed by a specific processor. In other applications such modularity may not be self evident or there may be more than one way of identifying parallelism. Software modularity in a sense implies an extension of the concepts of structured programming.

Once a modular structure is defined, then a processing environment is required where these modules are able to interact. Modules are also activated and deactivated as needed. One module can activate another in a different site. This requires a distributed control mechanism. The atomicity of execution means the fineness of individual operations performed by each module. Thus a module can be a very small item or a large program performing a complex operation. Identification of smaller modules means there is more chance of discovering identical operations and parallelism, and more opportunity to share modules. This, on the other hand, requires greater overheads when the interaction of individual modules are considered.

Granularity, another concept related to modules, refers to the amount of independent execution required before a module needs to interact with another one. The finer the granularity, the more calls are made to the communication substructure.

There is general agreement that the communication structure is to be defined independently of the modules or operating system aspects. It is then desirable that two processes should communicate in the same way irrespective of where they are located, i.e. in the same processor or not. Similarly, other interactions such as modules call for operating system functions to be independent of location. The communication system should also serve for kernel-to-kernel interaction. Finally, the invocation mechanism must be independent of logical processing units and geographical location. This leads to the same structure being used for both communication and invocation, i.e. sending and receiving messages. To achieve universality, the communication system must be transparent for the above processes.

Interaction via communication requires the definition of standard interfaces through which a process has access to the communication infrastructure. Security considerations necessitate there being certain safeguards for messages received. For example, the validity of all messages received needs to be checked. The messages sent could also be checked for validity. Such controls could be anything from a simple check of syntax to more sophisticated semantic checks.

Process–processor allocation and resource sharing are important aspects in operating system design. They require accurate knowledge of dependency of tasks on sites, whether or not multiple copies of modules are maintained, and the active state of processors. Shifting a code from one site to another may require adequate channel capacity.

Some Proposed Structures

As explained above, there is general agreement for structuring software in terms of independent modules. The formalism to achieve this, however, varies according to the implementation proposed. Here we will describe some of these proposals briefly.

Concurrent Pascal

The concept of *process* was introduced in conjunction with Concurrent Pascal, a language extension of Pascal destined for concurrent program development, in particular for writing operating systems software [7, 8]. A process is a self-contained sequential program with its own data, as shown in Fig. 6.1. Thus a process can access its own private data but cannot operate on data belonging to other processes. Also no other process can have access to its private data. To enable certain data structures to be shared, Concurrent Pascal uses the monitor structure [9]. The access rights shown in Fig. 6.1 refer to shared data on which it can operate.

A monitor defines a shared data structure and all the operations that can be performed on it. A monitor is a static entity and it can be activated by processes calling monitor procedures which form part of the monitor. A monitor also defines an initial operation which is executed once when the data structure is created. A monitor structure is illustrated in Fig. 6.2. A

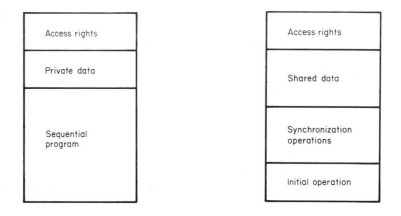

Fig. 6.1   Concurrent Pascal process.   *Fig. 6.2*   Concurrent Pascal monitor.

monitor can be used as a synchronization structure for concurrent processes and transmit data between them. Processes cannot operate directly on shared data; they can only call monitor procedures which in turn access the shared data. To ensure consistency, the monitor structure enforces exclusive access by executing one procedure at a time. If another call comes while a procedure is being executed, the calling process is delayed. For hierarchical design, monitor procedures can have access to other system components.

Concurrent Pascal also defines a third structure which is called a class. This is a data structure with possible operations on it which cannot be called simultaneously by several other components.

Processes, monitors, and classes with access rights enable us to construct directed graphs which help to visualize how concurrent processes interact. For example, Fig. 6.3 illustrates the message handling in a VTM node as a Concurrent Pascal systems graph.

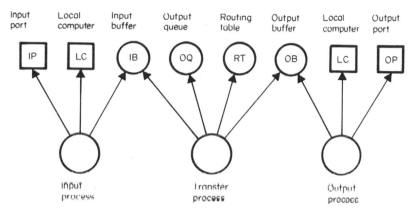

Fig. 6.3   Concurrent Pascal graph of VTM message-handling.

DEMOS

Although Concurrent Pascal was developed for multiprogramming for mono-processors, the DEMOS multi-microprocessor system is an example of this language being used for operating system development and application support [10]. DEMOS-86, developed by the National Physical Laboratory and Scicon Ltd., UK, links two to 16 Intel 8086 microprocessors into a single machine using a parallel communication bus 16-bits wide, with a speed of 1·5 Mbit/s line. DEMOS software programs are initially written in Pascal. Their interaction, however, is controlled by the underlying Concurrent Pascal environment. This enables them to communicate and have access to lower level facilities. Application programs then are independently compiled and loaded from disc as required. The run time modules derived from Concurrent Pascal programs are independent, have well-defined interfaces, and interact solely using a procedure call mechanism. A system generation program allocates compiled modules to processors in a static manner. The interaction between Concurrent Pascal modules at separate processors is achieved by communication. These messages carry the parameters of procedure call and returns. The inter-computer communication is managed by a small kernel executive resident in each processor. These kernels are identical, except features handling different peripherals are attached to different processors. The DEMOS kernel is written in PLM/86, Intel's systems implementation language with time-critical section written in 8086 assembler. A kernel, one copy of which resides in each microcomputer, is the heart of DEMOS. The collection of kernels are designed to co-operate and exchange information to emulate a single Concurrent Pascal virtual machine. Each kernel manages inter-computer communication and provides run-time support to local Concurrent Pascal program components. This includes scheduling simultaneously active processes, controlling access to monitor procedures, and handling device input–outputs. In short, the kernel provides an interface between a DEMOS Concurrent Pascal program and the base machines on which the program runs. The kernel's devices are invoked by software or hardware interrupts. Hardware interrupts originate conventionally from input–output devices, including the intercomputer communication system. Software interrupts originate in the Concurrent Pascal program. Program monitor calls, for example, cause the compiler to generate code for the appropriate software interrupt. DEMOS kernel utilizes the class construct so as to understand its functioning better. The kernel also handles the scheduling and the execution of concurrent processes on the machine. A scheduling algorithm allocates priorities to processes dynamically, giving highest priority to those processes which could degrade the performance of the system–input–output or are in control of a monitor. However, the algorithm also ensures that no process is starved of running time.

The kernel controls access to a monitor by implementation of FIFO queues in which processes wait until it is their turn to use the monitor. While a process is waiting, the kernel ensures that it is not scheduled to run, and once a process has finished using a monitor, the kernel adds it to the queue of processes to be rescheduled.

MICROS

MICROS is another distributed operating system developed at the State University of New York USA, which relies heavily on Concurrent Pascal constructs [11]. The MICRONET reconfigurable network computer is controlled by the MICROS distributed operating system. MICRONET and MICROS are offered as one solution to the twin problems of how to use VLSI modules to build extensible network computers of thousands of nodes, and how to manage large, distributed computers efficiently.

Each node in MICRONET consists of an LSI-11 host computer with 56 kbytes of local memory, linked by a DMA interface to a special packet-switching front-end computer with 64 kbytes of memory. Each node has external connections, at most, to two high-speed ($0 \cdot 5$ Mbyte/s) shared network communication buses, one fast peripheral storage device, and a few slow serial peripheral terminals.

Dual bus ports allow each node to be linked into loosely coupled networks in which message delays increase no faster than the logarithm of network size, even for very large number of nodes. Logic to control the shared network buses is distributed equally over all nodes attached to each bus. Because nodes are connected by passive wiring, network communications are inexpensive.

The MICROS distributed operating system is designed to control network computers of thousands of nodes for users simultaneously running a varying mix of large and small multicomputer tasks. For large networks, MICROS forms a hierarchy of nested network resource pools, managed by tasks running in nodes empirically selected to pass control messages efficiently. MICROS modules are written in Concurrent and Sequential Pascal for the LSI-11 and Z80 machines in each node.

Each node has a resident private copy of concurrent processes that handle input–output devices, execute sequential tasks, interpret task spawning commands, manage files and interprocess messages, and pass internodal messages using packet-switching protocols on the shared communication buses. Sequential program files for user and system tasks are dynamically loaded in each LSI-11 as needed.

There is a common message interface for communication among resident processes and dynamically loaded tasks, whether in the same or different nodes. Buffer pools, called channels, can be selected to manage high-volume data transmissions, as during file accessing. Users and tasks can spawn pipes of tasks executed in parallel and linked by channels.

CHORUS

The CHORUS project developed by INRIA, France, proposes an actor as the elementary processing unit [5]. An actor is a local entity, i.e. belonging to only one site at at time, composed of code and data. It can perform actions on local objects. It can also send and receive messages to and from other actors (either local or remote). A distributed application is a set of communicating actors.

The execution of an actor is controlled by the local operating system. An actor can call the operating system through primitives. The structuring in actors applies also to the operating system: a kernel (which is kept to a minimum) performs the basic operations; most operating system oriented functions are performed by actors.

Actors send and receive messages and also process them. For the sake of simplicity, each actor processes only one message at a time, without any possibility of being interrupted while doing so. Parallelism, if required, can be obtained using several actors. Actors can be considered as simply sequential message processors.

The processing of a message then forms a natural step in the execution of an actor. Various methods (the commitment in algorithms to the consistency of shared data, to group the messages sent at the end of a processing step, etc.) may help in achieving atomicity in the execution.

Moreover, the execution of the processing step can be started only by the reception of a message; the various actors of a distributed application can use this property to synchronize their executions.

With this architecture, an application can be described as a set of actors triggered by messages.

The processing structure described above suggests the following invocation mechanism: if an actor realizes some function in the system (either the application or operating system), it will perform this function on the reception of some particular message. Conversely, an actor which needs to realize a particular function sends a message to a specific actor which receives it and sends a response as another message. This does not prevent a function being written in a language using the procedure call, but these calls are not visible in the execution environment.

The invocation mechanism, in fact, consists of the sending of messages. This mechanism respects two conditions.

1. If two functions are realized by the same actor, the invocation of one by the other will lead to the sending of a message from the actor to itself; if two functions are realized by two actors, the invocation will lead to the sending of a message from one actor to another.
2. The sending of a message can be performed locally or remotely: the invocation mechanism is independent of the location of the function.

In CHORUS, a special feature related to this invocation mechanism, the switch procedure, is defined. As seen above, an actor can realize more than one function. Each of these functions is designed by its entry-point in the actor's code. When a message is received by an actor, the switch procedure permits the kernel to determine which entry-point must be entered to process the message.

Guardian Construct

A *guardian* is another construct proposed to achieve modularity [12]. A guardian consists of objects and processes. A process is the execution of a sequential program. Objects contain data. These are accessed and possibly modified by processes. Examples of objects are data items (integer, array, etc.), queues, and procedures. Objects are assigned types and only operations of the same type are permitted.

A computation consists of one or more guardians. Within each guardian, the actual work is performed by one or more processes. The processes within a single guardian may share objects, and communicate with one another via these shared objects. Processes in different guardians can communicate only by messages.

A guardian exists entirely at a single node of the underlying system. Thus a guardian is entirely in charge of its address space and storage management. All objects on the memory devices of this node and its processes run on the processor of the node. During the course of a computation, the population of guardians will vary. New guardians will be created and existing ones may self-destruct. The node at which a guardian is created is the node where it will exist for its life time. It must have been created by a guardian (a process) of that node. Each node comes into existence with a *primal* guardian which can, among other things, create guardians at its node in response to messages arriving from guardians at other nodes. This restriction on the creation of new guardians helps preserve the autonomy of the physical nodes.

A guardian is an abstraction of a physical node of the underlying network. It supports one or more processes sharing private memory, and communicates with other guardians only by sending messages. In the guardian, activity is local and hence requires less overheads. Each guardian acts as an autonomous unit, guarding its resource and responding only to authorized requests.

Medusa

Medusa is a multi-user operating system developed for Cm*, a multi-microprocessor system built at Carnegie-Mellon University [13]. Medusa is the second operating system for Cm*. The first system, StarOS [14, 15], has been concerned with making Cm* programmable at a high level by users. Medusa emphasizes the problems of structure, rather than facilities, and tries to gain an understanding of how to build distributed operating systems and exploit the hardware to produce a system organization with the following three attributes: (1) modularity, (2) robustness, and (3) performance.

The software organization required to achieve the above goals has been strongly influenced by the Cm* architecture. Two general attributes of Cm* have been especially important. First, the physical arrangement of the hardware components is a distributed one. For each processor there is a small set of local resources that is accessible immediately and efficiently: the other facilities of the system are also accessible, but with greater overheads. The second attribute is the power of the interprocessor communication facilities, which permits the efficient implementation of a variety of communication mechanisms ranging from shared memory to message systems. The combination of distribution and sharing of hardware gives rise to two corresponding software issues: partitioning and communication. The structure of Medusa has two significant characteristics:

1. The control structure of the operating system is distributed. The functionality of Medusa is divided into disjoint utilities. Each utility executes in a private protected environment, and implements a single abstraction for the rest of the system. Utilities communicate using messages.

2. Parallelism is implicit and expected in Medusa. All programs are organized as task forces, each of which is a set of co-operating activities. This makes it possible for very fine-grain interactions to occur within a task force. Each Medusa utility is a single task force.

Medusa discards the assumption that all operating system codes may be executed from any point in the system. A simplified example of this is depicted in Fig. 6.4. The operating system is divided into disjoint utilities. Utilities are distributed among the available processors, with no guarantee that any particular processor contains a copy of the code for any particular utility. Furthermore, to avoid contention or memory access delays, a given processor is permitted to execute a code for a particular utility only if it can do so locally.

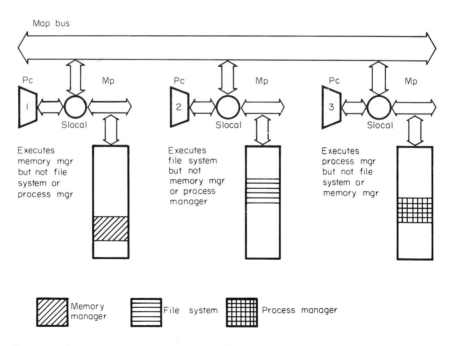

Fig. 6.4   The organization of Medusa.

Since no processor is guaranteed to be capable of executing any particular piece of utility code, it may be necessary for a program's flow of control to switch processors when it invokes utility functions. Trap or subroutine call instructions can not be used for invocation because they are incapable of crossing processor boundaries. In Medusa, messages provide a simple mechanism for cross-processor function invocation. If one program wishes to invoke a function of another it does so by sending a message to a particular pipe.

The invocation message contains parameters for the function invocation, as well as an indication of a return pipe: the return pipe is analogous to a return address for a subroutine call. The destination program receives the message, performs the requested operation, and sends a return message (containing result values) to the return pipe indicated in the invocation message. This message transaction is equivalent in power and effect to a call-by-value-result procedure invocation, with two major differences. First, the message crosses protection boundaries as well as processor boundaries, so that the invoker and server may exist in disjoint execution environments. Second, the invoker need not suspend execution immediately to await the requested service; if it has other functions to perform it may execute them concurrently with the execution of the server. The duality between messages and procedure calls has been discussed in more detail elsewhere [16].

The task force is the definition of a structure to support concurrency at the system's lowest level. It is defined as a collection of concurrent activities that co-operate closely in the execution of a single logical task. Activities are the entities that actually get scheduled for execution on processors. They are roughly analogous to processes or programs in other systems except that they exist only as part of a task force. A purely serial program is a degenerate task force with only one activity. All programs, including the operating system utilities, are task force.

When a task force is created, its activities are allocated statically to individual processors. In general, each of the activities of a task force will be allocated to a different processor; individual processors may be multiplexed between several activites belonging to different task forces.

In addition to its activities, a task force contains a collection of objects that may be manipulated by those activities. There are several types of objects in Medusa, each with its own set of type-specific operations. Access to objects is obtained through descriptors that are kept in protected objects called descriptor lists. The various types of objects may be divided into three general classes according to where the operations upon the objects are implemented. The simplest class consists of page objects: these may be associated with any of sixteen portions of an activity's 64 kbyte virtual address space and may then be read or written using memory references.

The second class of objects consists of pipes and semaphores, whose implementations are managed by Kmap microcode. Pipes and semaphores are protected. The third class of objects, containing file control blocks, task forces, descriptor lists, and others, is implemented by the operating system utilities. User programs make requests to the utilities in order to perform operations upon these objects.

There are two reasons for implementing the task force notion as a low-level system structure. First, most of the operating system functions are provided by task forces, hence the structure must exist at the operating system level. Second, for activites within a task force to interact on a fine grain, certain guarantees must be made to the task force. Foremost among these is the notion of co-scheduling which, if not provided by the operating system, cannot be implemented using higher-level protocols. A task force is said to be co-scheduled if all of its runnable activities are simultaneously scheduled for execution on their respective processors. In large task forces whose activities interact frequently, it is often the case that the descheduling of a single activity can cause the whole task force to block on locks held by that activity. If the task force is not co-scheduled, a form of thrashing occurs that is very similar to the thrashing in early demand paging systems. The set of activities that must be executed together for a task force to make progress on its task is analogous to a process' working set in a paging system. If the operating system does not provide for co-scheduling of this "activity working set", there is no way to simulate it at user level short of disabling timesharing. Simple algorithms have been developed for task force allocation and scheduling in Medusa to maximize co-scheduling.

Almost all of the operating system functions are provided by a collection of five utilities. Each utility is a task force that implements one or a few abstractions for the rest of the system. The memory manager is responsible for the allocation of primary memory, and also aids the Kmap microcode in descriptor list manipulation. The file system task force acts as a controller for all the input and output devices of the system, and implements a hierarchical file system nearly identical to that of Unix operating system [17]. The task force manager creates and deletes task forces and activities, and provides some simple debugging functions. The remaining two utilities are an exception reporter and a debugger/tracer. When an exception occurs on a processor, the kernel of that processor reports this to the exception reporter. It is the responsibility of the exception reporter to communicate information about the exception to relevant parties.

The activities of the utility task forces are spread among the available processors, typically with no more than one utility activity per processor. Although no memory is shared between utilities, central tables and synchronization locks for a given utility are shared between all the activities of that utility. The Kmaps route messages from user activities to utilities when the user activities request services from the utilities (see below); the same scheme is also used for service requests made by one utility of another.

Pipes in Medusa are similar to those of Unix [17] in that they hold uninterpreted strings of bytes. The operation of Medusa pipes differs from that of Unix pipes in two important ways: (1) the integrity of messages in Medusa is insured by maintaining byte counts for each message and by permitting whole messages only to be read from pipes; (2) the identity of the sender of each message is made available to the receiver of the message. Descriptors may not be passed using the pipe mechanism; instead, descriptors are moved by the memory manager utility in response to requests issued via pipes.

In a system that used message transactions as a procedure invocation mechanism, the overheads involved in such transactions are of fundamental importance. The degree to which the system can be partitioned is limited from an efficiency standpoint by the cost of an interaction between components. The time required for a 5–10 word message interaction in Medusa is approximately the same as the time used in executing 30 LSI-11 instructions (roughly 250 microseconds).

A primary reason for the efficiency of the message mechanism is the treatment of the "pipe empty" and "pipe full" conditions. In a producer–consumer relationship between activities, it is unlikely that the producer and consumer will operate at exactly the same speed. The communication pipe will almost always be either empty or full and one of the activities will usually have to wait for the other. Virtually all existing operating systems reschedule a processor as soon as the current activity blocks on an empty or full pipe; this means that when the pipe becomes non-empty or non-full a second context swap must be executed to reactivate the now-runnable activity. Thus almost every interaction between activities results in processor context swaps. In uniprocessor systems the context swaps are necessary since only a single activity can be executed at a time; however, in a multiprocessor system the context swaps may become the efficiency bottleneck in the interprocess communication mechanism.

A mechanism is provided for Medusa that would permit interactions to occur on a substantially finer grain than that of a context swap. When an activity attempts to send a full pipe or receive from an empty pipe its execution is suspended until the operation can proceed. However, the activity does not relinquish its processor immediately. For a small interval of time, called the pause time and specifiable by the activity, the activity's processor remains idle with the activity loaded. If the activity becomes runnable within the pause time it is reactivated without incurring any context swaps. If the pause time is exceeded, then the processor reschedules itself to another activity. Note that if the time for which the activity is blocked is less than two context swap times, then the lost processor time due to the pause is less than the time that would otherwise have been wasted in context swaps.

6.3   Inter-process Communication

The software implementation for multi-microprocessor systems, whether for systems software or applications software purposes, requires an adequate communication infrastructure. In fact, as mentioned in the previous section, for many implementations the communication system is seen as the main mechanism for application program module interaction as well as interaction between an application program and operating system, and between modules of an operating system. Messages are used not only to transfer data, but also as an invocation mechanism to perform a variety of control functions.

Communication software at the lowest level ensures the proper operation of the communication hardware. This may involve a single bus access for

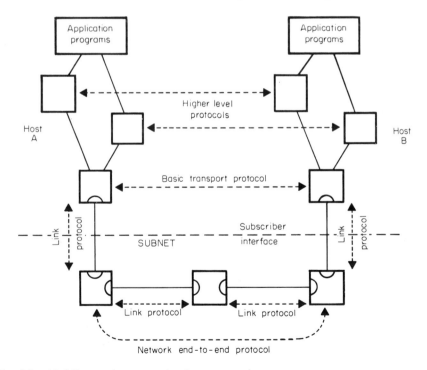

Fig. 6.5   Multilayered communication protocol.

a shared bus system or a multilayered protocol for a packed switched system, as shown in Fig. 6.5. In addition to error-free transmission, the communication software provides a link with the application and operating system software. The performance of the communication system is sometimes crucial for the performance of the overall system.

It is beyond the scope of this book to enter into the details of communications software [18]. Here it is worthwhile to present a few examples of how interprocessor communication is handled in certain multi-microprocessors, proposed or built.

DEMOS

In the DEMOS system, each component computer has an interface which transfers blocks of data directly between memory and the communication system. The access to this group bus consists of a microprocessor-based direct memory access controller. The kernel, introduced in the previous section, deals with intercomputer message transmission. In a DEMOS system, components of the Concurrent Pascal program which are on different machines communicate with each other through calls to, and returns from, monitor entry procedures, with data being passed as procedure parameters. Tables in each kernel contain information on the allocation of pieces of code to the various machines in the system, and these are used by the kernel in setting up messages. Because a process attempting to access a monitor may be delayed until the monitor is free (or until mutual exclusion has been relaxed), messages containing the parameters of a call on a monitor procedure may have to be queued. Doing this in a destination kernel may require too much space. Busy–waiting would waste communication bandwidth and might lead to individual starvation of access. Thus, transmission of a message is delayed until the successful completion of a handshake protocol conducted by the microprocessor in the group bus interface.

The first step in this protocol is the transmission of a Request-to-Send (RQTS) block to the destination kernel. RQTS blocks, which identify the calling and called instances, are placed by the destination group bus microprocessor in a storage area dedicated to the caller. When the requested monitor is free, it transmits a Go-Ahead (GA) block back to the caller's group bus microprocessor. This then transmits the parameters of the call to the destination as a DATA block. The contents of the DATA block are transferred into the workspace of the extension process assigned to execute the called monitor. For simplicity, a similar protocol is followed when returning result parameters even though the data space at the caller must always be available.

Although the overhead of the above protocol is small in terms of communication bandwidth, to reduce the overheads further, short messages are transmitted as SHORTDATA blocks which are handled and queued at the destination like RQTS. The length of message which can be included in a SHORTDATA block is set at system generation time, thereby allowing a trade-off between the block transfer execution overhead and static space allocation in each kernel.

The constituent computers of a DEMOS system are each connected to the intercomputer communication system by a hardware interface, the group bus interface. This is based on a microprocessor with a direct memory access (DMA) device. Under the control of kernel software the group bus transfers data between the store of the processor and the block transfer mechanism. It provides the computer with one output channel and one input channel.

To call a remote monitor, the kernel passes to the group bus interface the port number and channel number of the destination, and the address of a pointer block with a list of start addresses and subblock lengths which form the block to be transferred. The group bus interface retrieves the various subblocks from memory by direct memory access, transmits them, and interrupts the source processor.

The kernel associates the location of an area in memory with each input channel. When a block arrives, the group bus interface transfers it to this area by DMA and interrupts the destination processor.

RQTS and SHORTDATA blocks are of fixed sizes. The area in memory associated with their input channel can therefore also be of fixed size. Information from these blocks will be copied to its ultimate location by the kernel when necessary. Any DATA block must have been explicitly permitted by a GA block, so that its ultimate location is known in advance of its arrival. This location is the one associated by the group bus microprocessor with the appropriate input channel.

Not all DATA block transfers can proceed directly to or from the workspace of an instance because parameters do not necessarily occupy consecutive memory areas. The compiler can guarantee this only for the received parameters of a monitor call. In other cases the compiler produces a table of pointers to each contiguous subgroup of parameters. The group bus microprocessor makes direct use of this table to obtain from store the parameters to be sent.

The block transfer mechanism is a multiport communication system which connects to each computer via a group bus interface. It transmits arbitrary length blocks from port to port without individual starvation of any source. It has sufficient bandwidth to handle simultaneous use by a large number of computers, and shares this bandwidth fairly between them under high load conditions.

In DEMOS-86 this mechanism is implemented as a traditional computer bus, wide enough to transmit one 16-bit word, clocked at about 1·6 MHz rate. The bus consists of approximately 36 signal wires in a ribbon cable that provides access into each group bus interface (the length between each group bus being about two feet). Access to the bus is controlled by a bus arbiter.

The bus operates by the arbiter allocating the bus to a requesting port to allow a maximum number of words (packet) to be transferred to another port. The data words include control and address information. Blocks are segmented at the source port and transmitted packet by packet to the destination port. Each port can handle one incoming and one outgoing transfer at the same time. The transfers in progress could be either DATA blocks or control blocks, i.e. RQTS, GA, or SHORTDATA blocks. The message passing protocol and bus operation and arbitration ensures that all transfers, whether they are RQTS, GA, or SHORTDATA, are made within a finite time and in an orderly manner.

The arbiter protocol scans each port in a fixed order. When a port is found that requires service, it allocates the group bus for a packet transfer. At the end of the packet transfer, the arbiter frees the bus and continues its scan from the port just serviced. In this way each port obtains equal access to the group bus.

The group bus interface has been specifically designed so that a duplicated group bus can be implemented using one group bus interface control.

Various software strategies are possible with this hardware. In DEMOS-86, however, the system is used as two traffic-carrying buses. Each kernel passes some of its traffic over each group bus interface. If one bus fails, the group bus that remains operational takes all the traffic.

MICROS

In the MICROS system introduced in the previous section, information is passed between MICROS processes, whether in the same or different nodes, by sending messages which are contiguous blocks of data preceded by a header giving the source, destination, and length. All message texts within the same node are kept in a common message space monitor accessed by all local processes. Each process has a mailbox, which is a queue of pointers to messages that have been sent to it.

For processes in different nodes, the message text is transferred in packet-sized pieces over the DMA interface to the frontend buffers of the Z80 microprocessor. The source frontend routes the packets to the destination frontend, possibly via relays through other frontends if there is no external bus shared by both the source and destination nodes. At the destination, packets are stored in the Z80 memory until all parts of the original message have arrived. The assembled message is transferred by DMA into the message space monitor of the destination LSI-11.

Figure 6.6 gives a high-level overview of data flow within each MICRONET node controlled by MICROS. The circles represent about half the processes in each node. Pairs of processes are linked by monitors. One pair handles a user terminal (CRT) and acts as a dedicated command language interpreter (CLI) to spawn new tasks for the user. The other pair includes a CLI and a "task envelope" process which can dynamically load and run an arbitrary Sequential Pascal program to perform a requested system or user task. Tasks can issue commands to spawn additional tasks.

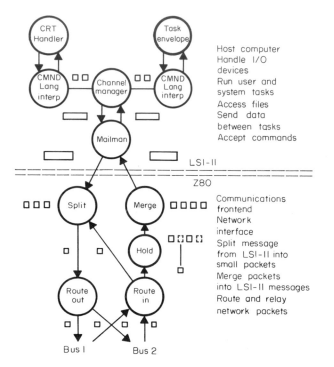

Fig. 6.6 Data flow among major processes of the MICROS operating system resident in each MICRONET node.

Monitors are omitted from Fig. 6.6. The arrows show the direction of data flow between the processes; the squares represent packets and short messages; the rectangles represent long messages. Figure 6.6 shows the passing of messages between LSI-11 processes as well as the splitting of outgoing messages into packets, and the merging of incoming packets into messages in the frontend.

Processes in the LSI-11 portion of each node may communicate by sending individual messages via the mailman process. The mailman routes messages to the mailbox monitors of destination processes in the same node. It queues messages for other nodes to be delivered via DMA to the frontend.

Whether in the same node or not, if two LSI-11 processes expect to exchange a large amount of data, they can request that a system of buffers, known as a channel, be established between them. Processes simply read and write data on channels. The monitors containing the channel buffers automatically send buffer-sized messages to move the data efficiently. A process accesses a disc file by setting up a channel involving a file manager process.

Messages leaving a node are split into packets when they are passed to the frontend. Individual packets are routed out of the node onto one of the attached buses whenever a bus is not busy. The immediate destination of each packet is either the final destination node if there is a direct bus connection or a relay node closer to the destination. Each frontend has a routing table giving immediate destinations for all final destinations that have recently been sent packets. If no routing is known, or all known routes have failed, a routing request message is sent up the hierarchy of management nodes which then determines an efficient route.

The frontend checks each entering packet to see whether it has reached its destination or whether it must be routed out on a relay to another node. To lessen buffer deadlock problems, whenever a packet is received that is part of a new message for the node, buffer space is reserved for all the packets in the message. As the rest of the packets for that message arrive, they replace the empty reserved spaces. When all packets have arrived, the linked list which they form is passed as a completed message to the mailman process for delivery to the destination process. The mailman lists all permanently resident Concurrent Pascal processes and all locally active Sequential Pascal tasks, as well as the "forwarding address" for each task which has recently been moved to another node, perhaps during error recovery. Packets sent to moved or non-existent tasks are forwarded or returned to the sender. Further details of the MICROS packet-switching subsystem have been discussed by Van Tilborn and Wittre [19].

To provide a uniform interface for sending data, whether over channels or by individual messages, there is a system of globally unique names used for all addressable entities in MICROS. These entities can be either the source or the destination for data. They include disc files, LSI-11 processes, Z80 processes, input–output devices, and Sequential Pascal tasks running in processes. All entities are processes or have handler processes associated with them. Data communication is the same regardless of the specific functions of the source and the destination, and whether they are in the same or different nodes.

The unique name for each entity has three fixed fields giving its type, creating node, and unique creation number within that node. A variable field tells which node was last responsible for the entity, and disc used for files which may migrate away from the peripheral storage device on which they were first created. Each unique name is 80-bits long and includes a 40-bit value assigned by the sequence number monitor in the creating node.

CHORUS

In the CHORUS project actors communicate by exchanging messages through ports [20]. A message is sent from one port of the sending actor torwards one (or several, i.e. broadcast) destination port(s) of the receiving actor(s). The transmission of a message is performed as a primitive offered by the kernel:

SEND (Source port, Destination port(s), Message);

Ports function only when associated with actors, i.e. a message destined for a port not associated with an actor will be lost. One port can be associated with only one actor at a time, but an actor can have several ports.

The establishment and release of an association between a port and an actor is performed as primitives offered by the kernel (an actor can open and close only its own ports):

OPEN-PORT (port);
CLOSE-PORT (port);

The concept of port decouples communication and processing. An actor is primarily interested in the functions being performed behind ports and not in the way these functions are performed. The usage of ports permits, for instance, the reorganization of actors which provide a function through a set of ports without the actors which use the function being aware of this reorganization, provided the global interface remains unchanged.

So ports provide a common interface both for the invocation and communication mechanisms. As the SEND primitive is independent of location, invocation and communication are also independent of location and of the communication subsystem.

A *send control procedure* and a *receive control procedure* are associated with each port; each time an actor executes a SEND primitive, the message is controlled twice: once with the second control procedure of the source port and once with the receive control procedure of the destination port. The first control is intended to control the external behaviour of the actor; the second is intended to protect the actor from unexpected messages. This decomposition of controls on communications into two parts (the sending and receiving sides) matches physical distribution and provides each site with its own autonomous protection.

A *linkage control procedure* is associated with each object: the first time an actor wants to access an object it must get a link to it; this is performed by issuing a primitive LINK; executing this LINK, the kernel uses the linkage control procedure in order to control whether or not the actor is entitled to access the object. Once the link has been established, the kernel does not necessarily control what the actor does to the object; the actor as a whole is supposed to behave correctly.

6.4   Language Considerations

High level languages and their translators have become essential for writing application programs for mono-processor systems. The same, however, cannot be said for multi-microprocessor systems. The immense variety of applications and hardware architectures, and the diversity of philosophies about how systems should be structured, makes it extremely difficult to design languages that are likely to be widely accepted. It still remains a difficult challenge to design a high level language which is sufficiently general and modular to accommodate a large number of architectural types of machines [21]. In the absence of bold and fresh ideas to express concurrency, it is then natural that current thinking is along the lines of extending or generalizing the sequential programming languages [22]. At least it is known that using this approach one has something that works for an isolated microprocessor which forms a constituent part of the whole system. Thus a sequential language enables individual software modules to be written. This is a rather primitive approach, however, where concurrency (which requires a control and communication structure), synchronization for resource sharing, efficiency and robustness aspects are outside the language consideration. A high level language is a medium which not only enables us to obtain a machine executable code but, perhaps more importantly allows us to formulate an application precisely. In this sense, there is a great vacuum for a vehicle to describe concurrent applications formally.

Another difficulty in using languages applicable to multi-microprocessor systems is the necessity for a translator. Translator writing immediately requires the specification of the target machine. It is desirable that the translator also runs on the target machine. Since there is no architectural uniformity, this requires a translator design which is capable of running on widely varying configurations. Ideally, a translator also should take advantage of the structure and hence be modular. This requires a significant departure from compiler writing for mono-processor systems.

A further difficulty stems from the fact that the language issues and run-time support aspects cannot be isolated totally. The attributes of the kernel are important in deciding whether or not certain issues need to be dealt with at the language level.

Most of the language proposals in the concurrent programming area also have an underlying model of distributed computing. The majority of these languages are in the research phase and many have not been implemented, so there is little hard practical experience. Most of the time the underlying model is not explicitly stated.

Even if one attempts to extract the underlying model from a proposal, it is not always an easy task. Sometimes the model and language issues become inseparable. The choice of a model would affect the programming methodology and the proof techniques for a language based on that model. A model provides a conceptual framework in which to discuss and understand the behaviour of concurrent computations, and is intended to capture the underlying philosophy of a programming language.

Some of the desired features of a concurrent language can be listed as follows [22].

Expressive power or richness This refers to the ability of the model/language in being able to express certain behaviours, i.e. the richness to be able to model certain computations like recursion, non-determinism, and so on. This property is also referred to as completeness or adequacy. An increase in expressive power is likely to be accompanied by an increase in the difficulty of proving programs. While it is desirable to have simplicity as one of the goals, it is not advisable to have that as the overriding criterion.

Provability One may be interested in proving many properties, like partial correctness, freedom from deadlocks, termination, fairness, etc. The presence of some constructs would make it extremely difficult, if not impossible, to prove certain properties. For example, at the current state of the art of program proving, the presence of time-outs could make the achievement of the tractability of proofs almost impossible. Of course, an important consideration is the power of the language used for specifying assertions about program properties. The assertion language or the logic used should be rich enough to be able to specify formally various desired properties [23].

Formalization of the semantics of constructs is an important prerequisite for program proving. While researchers have been discussing all of the above properties for a long time, there are very few well defined techniques or formal methods to illustrate the existence of the necessary properties.

Ease and efficiency of implementation   The implementation of certain features may be quite difficult to achieve. It is not sufficient merely to define primitives whose functionality makes them worth implementing. It must also be possible to deliver that functionality with reasonable efficiency. In most applications the efficiency, or costliness, is likely to be an important consideration. While some constructs might be implemented easily, the efficiency of such implementations may not necessarily be good. The practicality of mechanisms would be measured by the efficiency of their implementations.

Ease of use   The presence of powerful features does not mean that they would be easy to use. Normally high level constructs and good abstraction capabilities make things easier. Ease of use and expressive power are complementary criteria. A model/language being rich enough to express a certain type of computation does not automatically mean that it could be done in an easy way—certain ingenious, awkward and obscure ways have to be resorted to. Constructs which reflect intuitive ways of abstraction would be appealing to the user.

While writing programs, language primitives should allow coherent combinations. Avoiding subtle interactions among primitives would make them easier to use and help reduce errors. The flexibility of the constructs is also an important factor in the ease of their use.

Readability of resulting programs   Any proposal for new language features should be scrutinized closely to determine the effect of the proposed facility on program structure. The mechanisms should be such that they discourage complex and confusing structures. The presence of high level and very powerful constructs could lead to easily comprehensible programs. Of course, this may not always be the case. The ability to compose the process structure hierarchically should be of great benefit. In general, constructs that are easily verified are likely to be easily understood.

Impact of changes   If the constructs do not include or force a high degree of modularity, a change in the definition of one process may necessitate many changes throughout the rest of the system. This would be highly undesirable, particularly if the number of processes involved is quite large. Permitting a great degree of autonomy in the definition of processes would help a good deal in reducing and localizing the impact of changes.

Extent of concurrency possible   The greater the degree of concurrency the constructs permit to be expressed, the better. But the overheads involved in supporting such concurrency should not be such as to offset the advantages gained through the increase in parallelism.

The following is a brief description of the key features of various proposals that have been made in recent years.

Ada [24]

Ada has been developed by the US Department of Defence sponsorship essentially as a general purpose, high level language standard. To have as wide an application scope as possible, constructs have been introduced to help with concurrency.

For real-time applications, Ada provides facilities for multitasking, i.e. for logically parallel threads of execution that can co-operate in carefully controlled ways.

Tasks A task is an independent thread of execution. Like a package, a task is divided into a specification part and a body. Similarly, the modularity and abstraction concepts for packages generally apply to tasks. The task specification contains entry declarations that define the procedure-like calls that can be made to communicate with the task. The task body contains the code and variables—i.e. the internal state—which define the behaviour of the task.

Below is an example of a task to provide an asynchronous buffer between a line-oriented producer and a character-oriented consumer. This task declaration is assumed to be in the context of declarations of the types LINE and CHARACTER; the latter is, in fact, a predefined type.

```
task LINE-TO-CHAR is                         the task specification
   entry PUT-LINE (L : in LINE);
   entry GET-CHAR (C : out CHARACTER);
end LINE-TO-CHAR;
task body LINE-TO-CHAR is                          the task body
   BUFFER : LINE;
begin
   loop
     accept PUT-LINE (L : in LINE) do      the accept statement and its body
        BUFFER : = L;
     end PUT-LINE;
     for I in BUFFER'FIRST .. BUFFER'LAST loop
       accept GET-CHAR (C : out CHARACTER) do
         C : = BUFFER(I);
       end GET-CHAR;
     end loop;
   end loop;
end;
```

In this example, the task specification declares the entries PUT-LINE and GET-CHAR for use by other tasks. The body declares a local variable

BUFFER which is used to hold a complete line until all of its characters have been transmitted.

The code for the task consists of an unbounded loop with two basic parts. The first part is an accept statement for entry PUT-LINE. The accept statement looks quite similar to a procedure declaration; it has formal parameters and a body. The task waits at this point until some other task calls the entry PUT-LINE to provide data for the buffer. The second part is another loop that transmits one character at a time.

The above example illustrates the declaration of a single task object. Task types can also be declared, and any number of tasks of that type, i.e. all with the same properties, can be declared as objects. Indeed, because tasks are objects, they can be components of records or arrays. They can be pointed to by access objects, passed as parameters, created dynamically, and so on.

Intertask communication   When an entry has been called and the called task reaches an accept statement for that entry, a "rendezvous" is said to occur and only a single thread of execution is active for the duration of the accept statement. This single thread of execution can be thought of as belonging to either or both of the two tasks. At the end of the accept statement, the rendezvous is complete. Both tasks then continue independently and asynchronously.

In the last example given, when the task is waiting at PUT-LINE, a call on GET-CHAR is queued and the caller must wait. Conversely, when the task is waiting at GET-CHAR, a call to PUT-LINE is queued. Any number of tasks can be waiting for a given entry to be accepted. In this way, co-ordination is assured between tasks that provide lines and those that consume characters.

While the last example did not require more than one accept statement, there can be any number of accept statements for each declared entry. Other features allow accept statements to be executed conditionally.

A select statement allows a task to wait until a call is received on any one of a set of entries. If more than one call is waiting when the select starts, one of them will be chosen arbitrarily for processing.

The set of possibilities need not be the same on every execution of the select statement. An optional "when clause" evaluates the "true" condition for the entry to be "open", i.e. eligible to be accepted. If none of the alternatives are open and the optional else alternative appears in the select statement, it will be chosen. An exception is raised if no alternative is open and no "else" alternative is provided.

Other variations of the select statement include a delay or terminate alternative which can appear in place of an accept statement. However, neither a delay nor terminate alternative can be used in combination with the "else" alternative. If one of the alternatives of the select is a delay and there are no calls waiting for any of the open alternatives, the task will wait no longer than the specified amount of time before preceding. A delay value of zero means that if no entry call is immediately available, the task will not wait at all.

A terminate alternative is a particularly interesting construct that addresses the question, "How do you gracefully shut down a set of co-operating tasks without running the risk of error?" When a task is waiting at a terminate alternative, it effectively declares to the run-time environment that it is prepared to be terminated provided that all other tasks with which it can interact directly or indirectly are also at terminate alternatives or have completed. When all such tasks are in this state, none of the tasks of the set will ever receive an entry call (they are all waiting for some other task to make an entry call), so it is safe to terminate them all. Of course, if an entry call is received by a task that is prepared to terminate, the "okay-to-terminate-me" status is rescinded and normal processing resumes.

The language also supports a conditional entry call in which the calling task is not suspended and the entry call is not made unless the called task is ready to accept it immediately. There is also a timed entry call—a generalized form of the conditional entry call—in which the call is cancelled if it is not accepted within a specified amount of time. These two forms of entry call make it possible for a calling task to assure that it will not be indefinitely delayed by any task that it calls.

Priorities and scheduling   A task can either have a priority or not. A priority is specified by a pragma. If a priority is given, it must be a compile-time static value and cannot be changed during execution. When no priority is given, the compiler is free to choose when scheduling decisions need to be made, when the overhead of the scheduling decision can be avoided, and at what priority the task is run when it starts executing. The overhead of tasking in Ada is small. When implemented on a single processor, it is comparable to the overhead of procedure calls.

Interrupts   External devices are treated in Ada as tasks, and interrupts are treated as entry calls. The priority of the external device is dependent on its hardware priority and is guaranteed to be higher than any software priority. In this way, interrupts can be directly "connected" to accept statements. A consequence is that the tasking model is powerful enough to incorporate the conventional view of interrupts and interrupt handlers.

CSP [25]

A distributed program is defined as processes, with mutually disjoint address spaces, communicating directly using typed messages. Arrays of processes can be defined.

Sends and receives of messages are termed as input and output operations, respectively. Sender and receiver are to be synchronized for message transfer.

Non-determinism is permitted through guarded commands. Input statements can appear in guards. A parallel command permits the simultaneous initiation and execution of several processes.

PARLANCE [26]

A distributed program is obtained by processes communicating using messages through typed ports.

Hierarchies of processes can be defined, but only the processes of the lowest levels can have executable codes.

The minding of ports is done external to the process definitions. Each port of a process is connected to only one port or some other process. The bindings are static. Sender and receiver are to be synchronized for message transfer (input–output).

A parallel command which involves only input and/or output statements is permitted (i.e. AND-WAIT on multiple ports: all message transfers, in any order, must be completed before the command execution is deemed to be completed).

Non-determinism cannot be handled.

TASK [27]

TASK is an extension of BLISS and is based on the "object model" supported by the StarOS operating system for Cm*.

Different object types that exist are: task force, module, process, basic, stack, deque, device, mailbox.

A TASK specification affects only the creation and initialization of objects.

One codes algorithms in BLISS and specifies logical structures in TASK.

The language implements both procedure invocations and message-passing capabilities. A procedure invoked by a process could be executed in parallel with the execution of the caller. Communication is through mailboxes.

Dynamic definition and the creation of task forces are possible.

NSL [28]

NSL is a high level definition language used for specifying the detailed requirements on any particular layer or group of layers in the ISO model of a distributed system, i.e. a language for the specification of protocols.

Processes communicate through typed messagees. The dynamic creation of processes at a desired physical site/node of the network is possible. The destruction of a process by its creator is permitted, which results in the destruction of all its descendent processes.

Network data objects, like files, can be shared.

Certain protection mechanisms are provided.

PCL [29]

Distributed program components are processes, memory segments, ports, and links. Components can be in five states (uninstantiated, bound, expanded, initialized, and executing), and can be shared.

Ports are connected by links. Various types of links can be defined (including some performance attributes). The presence of a message at a port can be tested.

Highly dynamic process configurations can be instantiated during execution, using a static description of the process structure. Hierarchical structuring of processes (called clusters) is also possible. Process structure descriptions can be given in terms of static or structural characteristics, evolutionary characteristics, and creation characteristics.

Distributed Processes [30]

Processes contain local data, initialization statements, and common procedures, which can be called by other processes. Those calls are termed external requests.

Unsymmetric communication is implemented by procedure call semantics for message transmission.

The initial statements and external requests of a process are executed serially. They terminate or wait for some condition to become true. The execution of a process is similar to that of a monitor.

Guarded commands and guarded regions provide non-determinism. The latter can delay the execution of an operation.

An array of processes is possible.

Synchronizing Resources [31]

A distributed program consists of a set of resources, each of which encapsulates a set of processes and shared variables.

Processes contain declarations of externally callable operations (which are similar to the procedures of distributed processes and entries of Ada), which can have associated priorities.

Intra-resource process communication is done through operations on shared variables.

Inter-resource process communication is implemented through operations.

A multiprocess is a multiple number of those operations defined in a multiprocess which can be executed simultaneously.

Extended CLU [32]

A distributed program is achieved by one or more "guardians".

A guardian is a number of processes plus objects. Each guardian is expected to provide synchronization, security, backup, and recovery for the resources it protects. Each guardian exists entirely in a node of the underlying physical network.

Objects are passive; direct manipulation by processes is possible only through the invocation of predefined operations.

The dynamic creation of guardians is possible, but they are immovable from the nodes where they are created.

Inter-guardian communication exists only through messages. Time-outs are permitted in message reception statements, so that some exeption conditions can be handled.

Intra-guardian communication is achieved through shared objects.

Buffered messages are sent to typed ports. Compile time type checking can be quite comprehensive.

MOD [33]

MOD is derived from MODULA. Separate compilation is possible.

Processor modules contain processes and message types used by those processes. Variables can be shared by processes in a processor module, similar to the guardians in Extended CLU.

The network module links processor modules, and declares global types and constants.

The interface module is similar to monitor: mutual exclusion across all the contained procedures.

A process is initiated for every message.

Processes have dynamically variable priorities associated with them.

Extended POP-2 [34]

Extended POP-2 is, as the name implies, an extension of the artificial intelligence language POP-2.

Parameterized process types with input and/or output ports can be defined. Parallel processes (with connecting ports, either new and/or old ones) can be created dynamically, thus facilitating shrinking or expansion of process hierarchies.

Recursion is permitted, but non-determinism cannot be handled.

Ports are connected by channels. Each channel can have multiple readers (with only one writer) and all of them receive all the messages sent along the channel.

Actors [35]

A distributed program consists of dynamically creditable actors (which are somewhat like processes), communicating through buffered messages. Messages may transmit actors' names.

Non-determinism, recursion, and time-outs can be specified.

Serializers are used to control access to protected resources. The serializer mechanism is a generalized and improved monitor mechanism.

PLITS/ZENO [36]

A distributed program is obtained by multiple modules (which are similar to processes) communicating solely through buffered messages.

Modules can be created dynamically, but cannot be destroyed by other processes.

All components/fields of a message may not be visible to the recipient of that message. Module names, as well as transaction names, could be used for controlling message receptions and dispatches. Transaction names could be considered as dynamically created mailboxes.

Parts of PLITS/ZENO are intentionally not strongly typed.

Flowgraph [37]

A flowgraph is only a model, not a language.

Processes communicate through typed ports of channels, with unbuffered messages.

Recursion and non-determinism can be expressed.

Processes and channels can be created dynamically.

LIMP [38]

A distributed program consists of processes communicating solely through unbuffered messages.

Processes can be created dynamically.

Typed channels (possibly with multiple readers and writers) link processes for message transfers. The read capability for a channel is called a "source" and the write capability a "sink".

Channels, sources and sinks can be created dynamically and passed around in messages.

References

[1] S. Ziegler, N. Allegre, R. Johnson, J. Morris and G. Burns. Ada for the Intel 432 Microcomputer, *IEEE Computer*, **14**, No. 6, June 1981, pp. 47–56.

[2] Y. Paker. "Minicomputers, A Reference Book for Engineers and Managers", Abacus Press, London, 1981.

[3] D. A. Anderson. Operating systems, *IEEE Computer*, June 1981, pp. 69–82.

[4] D. C. Tsichritzis and P. A. Bernstein. "Operating Systems", Academic Press, London and New York, 1974.

[5] J. S. Banino, A. Caristan, M. Guillemount, G. Morisset and H. Zimmerman. The impact of distribution on operating system design, in "Locally Distributed Computer Systems", Edinburgh University and INRIA, September 1980.

[6] A. K. Jones, R. J. Chansler, Jr, I. Durham, P. Feiler and K. Schwans. Software management of C.m*—A distributed multiprocessor, *National Computer Conference*, 1977.

[7] P. B. Hansen. The programming language Concurrent Pascal, *IEEE Trans. on Software Engineering*, **SE-1**, No. 2, June 1975, pp. 199–207.

[8] P. B. Hansen. "Operating System Principles", Prentice-Hall, Engelwood Cliffs, N.J., July 1973.

[9] C. A. R. Hoare. Monitors: an operating system structuring concept, *Commun. Ass. Comput. Mach.*, **17**, October 1974, pp. 549–557.

[10] B. Brinkman, M. Dowson, B. McBride and G. Smith. "The DEMOS-86 Multimicrocomputer", Scicon Consultancy Int. Ltd., 49–57 Berners Street, London W1P 5AQ.

[11] L. D. Wittie and A. M. Vantilborg. MICROS, a distributed operating system for MICRONET, a reconfigurable network computer, *IEEE Trans. on Computers*, **C-29**, No. 12, December 1980, pp. 1133–1144.

[12] B. Liskov. Primitives for distributed computing, *7th Symposium on Operating System Principles*, Pacific Grove, California, December 1979.

[13] J. K. Ousterhout, D. A. Scelza and R. S. Sindhu. Medusa—An experiment in distributed operating system principle, Pasitre Grove, California, December 1979.

[14] A. K. Jones, R. J. Chansler, Jr, I. Durham, P. Feiler and K. Schwans. Software mangemet of C.m*—A distributed multiprocessor. *AFIPS—Conference Proceedings*, **46**, NCC, 1977, pp. 657–663.

[15] A. K. Jones, R. J. Chansler, Jr, I. Durham, P. Feller, D. A. Sceiza, K. Schwans and S. R. Vegdahl. Programming issues raised by a multiprocessor. *Proceedings of the IEEE*, **66**, No. 2, 1978, pp. 229–237.

[16] H. C. Lauer and R. M. Needham. On the duality of operating system structures, in *Proceedings of the 2nd International Symposium on Operating*

Systems, IRIA, 1978. Reprinted in *Operating Systems Review*, **13**, 2, April 1979, pp. 3–19.

[17] D. M. Ritchie and K. Thompson. The UNIX time-sharing system. *CACM*, **17**, No. 7, July 1974, pp. 365–375.

[18] D. W. Davies, D. L. A. Barber, W. L. Price and C. M. Solomonides. "Computer Networks and their Protocols", John Wiley and Sons, Chichester, UK, 1979.

[19] A. M. Tilborn and L. D. Wittre. Packet switching with concurrent pascal in a network computer, *IEEE COMPCON 80 Fall*, September 1980.

[20] R. M. Bulzer. PORTS—a mathod for dynamic interprogram communication and job control. *Proc. of the AFIPS Conference* 39, 1971.

[21] R. Bryant and J. Dennis. Concurrent programming, in "Research Directions in Software Technology", P. Wegner, Ed., The MIT Press, Cambridge, Mass.

[22] C. Mohan. A perspective of distributed computing: models, languages, issues and applications, writing paper DSG-8001, Department of Computer Sciences, University of Texas at Austin, Texas.

[23] M. Chandy and J. Misra. Distributed simulation: A case study in design and verification of distributed programs, *IEEE Trans. on Software Engineering*, September 1979.

[24] F. R. Brender and I. R. Nassi. What is Ada? *IEEE Computer*, June 1981, pp. 17–24.

[25] C. A. R. Hoare. Communicating sequential processes, *CACM*, August 1978.

[26] P. Reynolds. Parallel processing structures: languages, schedules, and performance results, Ph.D. thesis, University of Texas at Austin, 1979.

[27] A. Jones and K. Schwans. TASK forces: distributed software for solving problems of substantial size, *Proc. IV Int. Conf. on Software Engineering*, September 1979.

[28] F. Tarini, R. Sharp, M. Martelli and A. Endrizzi. A network system language, *Proc. I Int. Conf. on Distributed Computing Systems*, October 1979.

[29] V. Lesser, D. Serrain and J. Bonar. PCL: A process-oriented job control language, *Proc. I Int. Conf. on Distributed Computing Systems*, October 1979.

[30] P. Brinch Hansen. Distributed processes: a concurrent programming language, *CACM*, November 1978.

[31] G. Andrews. Synchronizing resources, Technical Report TR 78-368, Cornell University, February 1979.

[32] B. Liskov. Primitives for distributed computing, *Proc. VII Symp. on Operating Systems Principles*. December 1979. (Also Computation Structures Group Memo 175, MIT, May.)

[33] R. Cook. *MOD—A language for distributed programming, *Proc. of the I Int. Conf. on Distributed Computing Systems*, October 1979.

[34] G. Kahn and D. MacQueen. Coroutines and networks of communicating processes, *Proc. Information Processing*, IFIP, 1977.

[35] C. Hewitt, G. Attardi and H. Lieberman. Security and modularity in message passing, *Proc. of the I Int. Conf. on Distributed Computing Systems*, October 1979.

[36] J. Feldman. High level programming for distributed computing, *CACM*, June 1979.

[37] G. Milne and R. Milner. Concurrent processes and their syntax, *JACM*, April 1979 (Also Internal Report CSR-2-77, University of Edinburgh, February 1978.)

[38] J. G. Hunt. An introduction to LIMP: an experimental language for the implementation of messages and processes, *Proc. of the V Conf. on Programming Languages of the Gesselschaft Fuer Informatik*, Technische Universitaet Braunschweig (W. Germany), March 1978.

Further Reading

Hansen, P. B. Network: a multiprocessor program, *IEEE Trans. on Software Engineering*, **4**, No. 3, May 1978, pp. 154–155.

Hansen, P. B. Distributed processes: a concurrent programming concept, *Communications of the ACM*, **21**, No. 11, November 1978, pp. 930–941.

Hoare, C. A. R. and Perrot, R. M. "Operating Systems Techniques", Academic Press, London and New York, 1972.

Wirth, N. Toward a discipline of real-time programming, *Communications of the ACM*, **20**, No. 8.

Chapter 7

Reliability and Fault-tolerant Architectures

7.1   General Considerations

Since the early days of computers, it has been important to consider reliability problems in both the construction and use of these machines. Today, individual computers, or interconnected machines, are applied in vastly varying applications where in many cases the system depends critically on their reliability.* For example, computer controlled railway signalling would endanger human life if computer faults are allowed to disrupt the signal system. In industrial control unreliable computer operations may have catastrophic consequences. Computers also have to function where human intervention for maintenance or repair is either difficult or impossible such as in aviation or satellites. As mentioned earlier, there are systems where safety critically depends on reliable computer operation. Another example is future aircraft which will be inherently unstable and controlled by computers for better fuel efficiency. In such aeroplanes the pilot is excluded from the flight-stabilizing loop since no human intervention could be swift and precise enough to handle the advanced airframes of the 1990s. In such an aircraft, the computers are expected to break down less often than the wings are expected to fall off planes in flight [1].

In the most general sense reliable computing means the correct execution of a specified set of algorithms and encompasses all of the following elements [2]:

1. correctness and completeness of software specification;
2. testing and verification of programs;
3. elimination of hardware design errors;

*Reliability $R(t)$ is defined as the probability of a system operating fault free for t seconds.

4. continued correct execution of programs and protection of data in the presence of hardware failures;
5. security of the computing system against failure-induced disruption or deliberate invasion.

The need for long uninterrupted periods of reliable computing, especially in cases without external assistance by maintenance specialists, can be met by the complementary approaches of fault intolerance and fault tolerance.

Fault intolerance tries to assume the elimination of all the causes of unreliability. All the available technological and design know-how is applied to achieve this.

Fault tolerance is the approach which recognizes that hardware and software faults are inevitable and attempts to assume reliable computation by use of protective redundancy. The redundant parts of the system (both hardware and software) either take part in the computing process, thus contributing to overall performance in the absence of faults, or are present in a standby condition, ready to intervene when a fault occurs.

There are three main causes of faults in hardware systems:

1. permanent failures of hardware components;
2. intermittent malfunction of components;
3. external interference with computer operation.

In order to ensure that the above sources of faults do not affect the correct execution of programs, protective redundancy is introduced into a computer system in three forms:

1. additional hardware (hardware redundancy);
2. additional programs (software redundancy);
3. repetition of operations (time redundancy).

When special hardware is designed for fault tolerance, this, in principle, does not add any computational feature nor help with performance. There are two main approaches that can be adopted:

1. static hardware redundancy, and
2. dynamic hardware redundancy.

Static hardware redundancy is achieved by employing redundant components in a hardware module so that the terminal activity of the module remains unaffected in the presence of hardware failure so long as the protection is effective. This type of redundancy is also called "enabling" redundancy since the additional components ensure that a failure has no effect on the output and hence is masked from the actual operation. This technique, in fact, requires the parallel action of a component and its standby(s) so that a fault in the component goes unnoticed as the standby is activated automatically. Thus, the most commonly used techniques involve the replication of individual electronic components and triple modular redundancy with voting. This last method was originally proposed to build reliable machines from unreliable components [3].

In the dynamic redundancy approach, faults are allowed to occur and propagate a number of steps until a detection mechanism is activated which in turn activates an appropriate recovery action. Usually, this requires intervention of the software. If the cause of the fault can thus be eliminated, then we would have a self-repairing computer system.

Dynamic hardware redundancy can be introduced at various levels. Parity check, for example, is a commonly used method for data storage and transmission. At the other end of the spectrum, we have a complete computer system duplicated to provide redundancy. Thus it is an essential design aspect to use a modular structure. The modules, which are subcomputers, could have a very fine grain such as individual logical functions or a very coarse grain like complete processors or computers.

Fault detection can take many different forms, such as error codes, the duplication of operations, and so on. Error codes give a check of individual words. To check whether a module is executed fault free, a duplication of the module can be used. The execution of both modules are checked against each other and a discrepancy indicates a fault condition.

Upon the discovery of a fault, a recovery procedure takes place. This could be a restart of the program (roll-back), and if this fails a permanent fault is assumed. In this case, the failed module needs to be identified and replaced. Error correcting codes make it possible for computation to proceed if the number of faults does not exceed the power of correction of the code. Another approach is to "reconfigure" the system so that the faulty module is excluded from further operations. For example, if there is a memory failure, that particular module can be avoided.

Fault detection and recovery require that a "hard core" section of the computer functions properly to carry out the above operations. This can be done in a number of ways, such as by duplexing with supplementary supervision, triplication and voting, or permanently wired-in error correction codes. Another aspect of the hard core, is the restart of the computer from "cold start". If, for example, due to an emergency situation such as loss of power, the computation is interrupted, the hard core must have sufficient facilities to restart it.

Software redundancy includes additional programs, program segments and instructions to carry out the fault detection and recovery procedures. These are mostly used in conjunction with hardware redundancy. There are various approaches such as the multiple storage of critical programs and data, test and diagnostic programs, supplementing the executive program with features to help with fault tolerance. Software redundancy is attractive since it can be developed, extended, and altered without any modifications to the hardware available.

On the other hand, software redundancy is much less understood and the techniques less developed. One main drawback is the assumption of the correctness of the fault-tolerant software. It is almost impossible to ascertain that a given piece of software is "bug" free, and if there are multiple copies of the software the implication is that there are multiple copies of the "bug". Another important aspect is that when a fault occurs, in order for the software to handle fault detection and recovery it is necessary for there to be sufficient computation facility unaffected to run these programs correctly.

Time redundancy consists of repeating the execution of a module and checking results. This clearly works for transient faults and is not suitable for permanent faults.

Multi-processors bring in a new dimension in achieving fault-tolerant operation. First of all, the microprocessor architecture does not favour the hardware redundancy at circuit component or logic function level since a designer cannot penetrate inside a chip. That is the domain of VLSI designers, and any fault-tolerant techniques that they may use are masked from the operation at the pin level. Yet at the processor level, one can introduce redundancy in a natural and cost effective manner. That is why one approach has been to design multi-microprocessor systems to achieve computers of high availability (the probability that a system is operational at a given time) [4]. Another approach has been to use the redundancy that exists naturally in a distributed system to also provide spare capacity so that when one computer fails, another one comes to the aid in recovery. Uniprocessor systems have required specialized hardware for recovery. The redundancy that is inherent in a multi-microprocessor system makes this, by and large, unnecessary. Fault detection and recovery then, can make much use of software techniques. It is then possible for two microcomputers to run detailed diagnostics to check each other, locate faulty computers, and take them out of service. The overall effect is loss of performance, but the system could still be usable. This is called "graceful degradation" or "fail-soft" situation.

Different degrees of fault-tolerant design are considered according to the type of application concerned. The following application types can be differentiated.

Computation-critical applications   The most stringent fault tolerance requirements arise in real-time control systems in which faulty computations can jeopardize human life or expensive equipment. Such real-time applications require not only that a computation be correct, but also that any delay associated with fault recovery be very small (in the order of milliseconds). As computers take on more important roles in factories, hospitals, transportation systems, and other critical applications, the number of computation-critical applications will grow. A major programme in this area (sponsored by NASA) is the development of avionics computers for dynamically unstable aircraft, as mentioned above.

Long-life applications   Long-life systems are ones which are never maintained. Unmanned spacecraft are the most dramatic examples; manual repair is impossible and they must operate reliably for five years or more. Computer systems for these applications are highly redundant, providing enough spare hardware to maintain nominal performance until the end of a mission. Long-life systems may or may not perform critical computations. Some systems rely on remote ground-based fault diagnosis and external reconfiguration, while others provide on-board automated fault recovery.

Applications requiring high availability   In large, resource sharing systems, the occasional loss of one user's computations is acceptable, but a system-wide stoppage or the destruction of a common data base is unacceptable. Examples are telephone switching computers and a variety of commercial timesharing devices.

Signal processing applications   High-performance computing systems will reach a point of speed and complexity where expected performance cannot be achieved without the use of fault tolerance. Super-computers are moving toward this limit, as can be seen in the four-hour MTBF of the Cray-1. The introduction of submicron VLSI technology, coupled with signal processing applications being studied by NASA and DoD in the USA, will increase system complexity by one or more orders of magnitude beyond the current super-machines. For example, a proposed synthetic aperture radar processor requires an array of 1000 processing elements, each with a complexity equivalent to 40 000 gates. In such systems, transient errors due to complexity and limited clock margins, can be frequently expected, along with a relatively high permanent failure rate.

Maintenance postponement   In a number of applications the life-cycle cost of unscheduled maintenance can be higher than the cost of fault tolerance. This is especially true for some military systems which must have many repair staff assigned to them. In an environment where on-site repair is expensive, fault tolerance becomes attractive. If, after a fault occurs, a computer system can continue operating while a defective module is shipped to a central repair facility, the number of "front line" repair staff can be reduced, along with their associated test equipment (which can also fail).

VLSI technology should become sufficiently reliable so that, for a modest amount of redundancy, it may be possible to postpone on-site repair of small computing systems for their entire operational lives.

7.2   Hardware Redundancy

There are a wide variety of ways in which hardware redundancy can be introduced. A multi-microprocessor system is inherently hardware-redundant since it includes more than one processor. Such a system could be designed with fault-tolerant considerations being of primary importance or to satisfy other application requirements. That there is built in hardware redundancy in multi-microprocessor systems, however, allows the introduction of fault-tolerant aspects in a cost-effective manner by adding small amounts of hardware and the appropriate software.

Hardware redundancy can be introduced in the subsystem of a multi-microprocessor so as to protect these parts against possible faults. For example, error detection and correction codes can be introduced to protect memory or communication lines. With VLSI technology, the application of such techniques could be quite straightforward.

A more sophisticated approach involves redundancy in the main communication system, e.g. by duplicating the main processor bus or providing alternative routes in a loosely coupled system.

When local redundancy is provided for fault detection and correction, then when a fault occurs which can be handled by the extra hardware, the computation goes on unaware of the fault. To handle permanent faults, means must be devised so as to inform the fault-handling software that there is a fault in a given piece of equipment even though computation can go on unaffected. This could result in a message for a maintenance engineer or the isolation of a faulty component and its replacement in applications where human intervention is possible.

The use of a federation of microprocessors to obtain highly reliable computers is an area of great interest in which a number of approaches have been proposed. One such project is the C.vmp, a voted multiprocessor developed at Carnegie-Mellon University [5].

C.vmp

The C.vmp was designed to satisfy certain design goals.

1. *Permanent and transient fault survival*   The system should have the capability of continuing correct operation in the presence of a permanent hardware failure, i.e. a component or subsystem failure, and in the presence

of transient errors, i.e. if a component or subsystem is lost for a period of time due to the superimposition of noise on the correct signal.

2. *Software transparency to the user*   The user should not know that he is programming a fault-tolerant computer, with all fault tolerance being achieved in the hardware. This would allow the user to rely on established software libraries, increasing the reliability of the software itself.

3. *Capable of real time operation*   A fault should be detected and corrected within a short period from the time the fault actually occurs.

4. *Modular design to reduce down-time*   The hardware should be able to operate without certain sections activated. Hence, maintenance could be performed without having to halt the machine. Modularity includes the design of a separate power distribution network so that selected sections of the machine can be de-activated. The use of modules in the design also has the virtue of allowing the user to upgrade in steps from a non-redundant, to a fully fault-tolerant computer.

5. *Off-the-shelf components*   To decrease the amount of custom designed hardware, to be able to rely on an established software library, and to enable systematic upgrading to a fault-tolerant system, the computer should primarily employ off-the-shelf components. Thus, advantage can be taken of the greater reliability of high production volume components.

6. *Dynamic   performance/reliability   trade-offs*   The   fault-tolerant computer should have the capability, under operator or program control, dynamically to trade performance for reliability.

System architecture

To be consistent with the design goals of modularity and software transparency, bus level voting has been selected as the major fault-tolerance mechanisms, i.e. voting occurs every time the processors access the bus to either send or retrieve information. There are three processor–memory pairs, each pair connected via a bus, as shown in Fig. 7.1. C.vmp is in fact composed of three separate machines capable of operating in independent modes executing three separate programs. Under the control of an external event or under the control of one of the processors, C.vmp can synchronize its redundant hardware, and start executing the critical section of code.

With the voter active, the three buses are voted upon and the result of the vote is sent out. Any disagreement among the processors will, therefore, not propagate to the memories and vice versa. Since voting is a simple act of

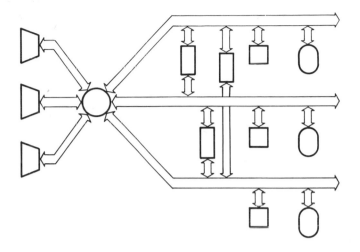

Fig. 7.1   C.vmp configuration.

comparison, the voter is memoryless. Disagreements are caught and corrected before they have a chance to propagate. The non-redundant portion of the voter does not represent a system reliability bottleneck, as will be shown later. However, the voter may be totally triplicated if desired. Even with voter triplication the voter can have either a transient or a hard failure and the computer will remain operational. In addition, provided that the processor is the only device capable of becoming bus master, only one bidirectional voter is needed regardless of how much memory of how many input–output modules are on the bus. Voting is done in parallel on a bit by bit basis. A computer can have a failure on a certain bit in one bus, and, provided that the other two buses have the correct information for that bit, operation will continue. There are cases, therefore, where failures in all three buses can occur simultaneously and the computer would still be functioning correctly.

Bus level voting works only if information passes through the voter. Usually the processor registers reside on the processor board and so do not get voted upon. Thus this approach does not provide protection against failures in internal registers. However, since processor registers are stored or loaded to or from memory, and hence through the voter, this would result in their eventual detection. One study [6] shows that, on average, for the PDP 11 processor a register gets loaded or stored to memory every 24 instructions, a subroutine call occurs every 40 instructions which saves the program counter on stack, and the only register which is not normally saved or restored is the stack pointer. The stack pointer then needs to be stored and loaded periodically so as to maintain fault-tolerance.

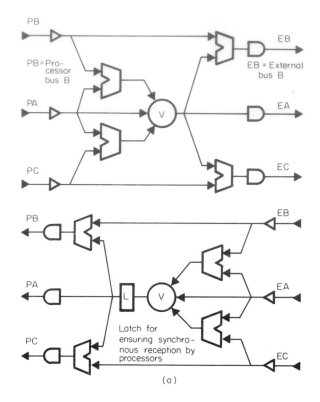

Fig. 7.2a   C.vmp unidirectional voter multiplexing.

The multiplexed paths through the voter are shown in Fig. 7.2. Figure 7.2a shows the case for the (unidirectional) control lines. Signals generated by the processor are routed from bus receivers to multiplexors which allow either signals from all three buses, or signals only from bus A, to pass to the voting circuit. The output of the voting circuit always feeds bus drivers on external bus A, but is multiplexed with the signals initially received on buses B and C. This arrangement allows all three processor signals to be voted on and sent to all three external buses; the signal from only processor A to be broadcast to all three external buses; and the independent processor signals to be sent to the separate external buses, albeit with extra delay on bus A.

Figure 7.2b shows the more complex case of bidirectional data/address lines. Two sets of bus transceivers replace the sets of receivers and transmitters used before, and another level of multiplexing has been added. The signals received from both sets of transceivers are fed into a set of multiplexors that choose which direction the signals are flowing. After passing through the set of multiplexors and the voter circuit, the voted

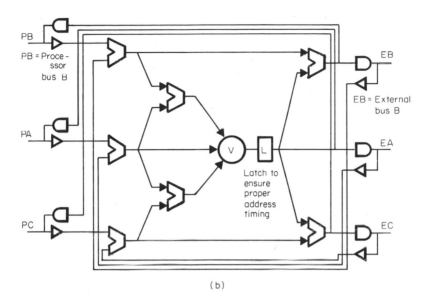

(b)

Fig. 7.2b   C.vmp bidirectional voter multiplexing.

signal goes through a latch which ensures that bus timing specifications are met. From there the signals pass onto the opposite bus from which they were initially received. (Note that the drivers on the receiving bus are disabled to avoid both sinking and sourcing the same signal.)

Voting mode   The transmitting portion of each of the three buses is routed into the voter, and the result of the vote is then routed out to the receiving portion of all three buses. In addition to the voting elements the voter has a set of disagreement detectors. These detectors, one for each bus, are activated whenever that bus has lost a vote. By monitoring these disagreement detectors, one can learn about the kinds of failures the machine is having.

Broadcast mode   Only the transmitting portion of bus A is sampled, and its contents are broadcast to the receiving portions of all three buses. This mode of operation allows selective triplication and non-triplication of input–output devices, depending on the particular requiremens of the user. The voter has no idea which devices are triplicated and which are not. The only requirement is that all non-triplicated devices be placed on bus A.

Independent mode   Buses B and C are routed around the voting hardware. Bus A is routed to feed its signals to all three inputs of the voting elements. In this mode C.vmp is a loosely coupled multi-processor. Switching between independent and voting modes allows the user to perform a performance/reliability trade-off.

The unidrectional control signals generated by devices on the external buses are handled in the same way as processor signals, except that the direction (external-processor) has been changed.

Peripheral devices

In most cases, to triplicate a device simply requires the standard boards being plugged into the backplane, as is the case with memory. In some cases, however, the solution is not quite so simple. One example of a device that has to be somewhat modified is the floppy disc drive. The three floppy discs run asynchronously. Therefore there can be as much as a 360 degree phase difference in the discettes. Since the information does not arrive under the read heads of the three floppy discs simultaneously, the obvious solution is to construct a buffer which is large enough to accommodate the size of the sectors being transferred.

The main synchronization problem is to find out when all three floppy discs have completed their tasks or when one of the floppy discs is so out of specification that it can be considered failed. Once this is determined the "DONE" signals are transmitted to the three buses simultaneously.

In systems like C.vmp, where all processors must be tightly synchronized with respect to the processor clock, a single clock to drive all the processors and voter circuits is required, as shown in Fig. 7.3. Even a several

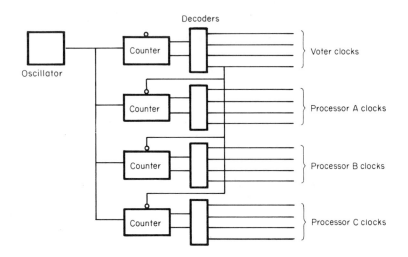

Fig. 7.3   C.vmp processor clock synchronization.

nanosecond difference is of significant magnitude for pulses that last less than 100 ns, causing discernible disagreement at the voter. Thus the processes have to be identical and identically loaded, and located at close physical proximity. It should be mentioned that the oscillator in Fig. 7.3 is a non-redundant component, in which a fault completely cripples the system. Thus special attention is required to make the oscillator as fault-intolerant as possible. Of course, such hard core items as an oscillator and power supply can be designed to be fault-tolerant, for example, by duplication [7].

Fault-tolerant Microprocessor (FTMP)

A design sponsored by NASA is the FTMP, the Fault-Tolerant Micro-processor developed by the C.S. Draper Laboratory [4] based on earlier work [8]. The objective is to achieve a failure probability of 10^{-9} for a ten hour flight necessary for the design of dynamically unstable commercial aircraft.

FTMP employs fully synchronous hardware partitioned into individually reconfigurable processor/cache, memory, and input–output modules. These are connected by common bused clock and data lines, and employ serial bit-by-bit voting in each processor/cache and each memory module. Dual "bus guardian" submodules control access to the buses to prevent bus pollution by "babbling" transmitters; they are also used to reconfigure module assignments. The processor/cache and memory modules are

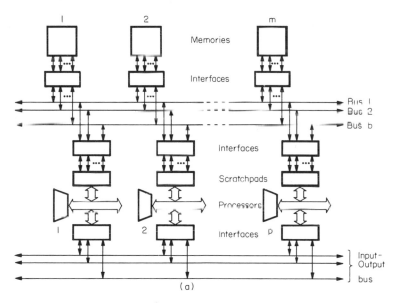

Fig. 7.4a   FTMP symmetric configuration.

configured into "triads" (groups of three processors and memories), each of which is a voting set. Each triad carries out an independent computation, and the collection of triads makes up a multiprocessor.

In this configuration, replication and voting are used almost exclusively to locate errors and to mask them for a short time until it is convenient to reconfigure (Fig. 7.4a). Reconfiguration is wholly software directed. Failed units are retired and replaced with spares, until all spares have been exhausted. There are three categories of units that are so treated: processor-scratchpad units, memory modules, and buses. All mechanisms that are needed for fault tolerance can be routinely tested to uncover lurking faults. A lurking fault is one that causes no error itself, but which can foil recovery after a second fault.

Processor triads

Processing units (i.e. processor–scratchpad units) are assigned to groups of three, called processor triads. The three members of a triad operate in bit synchronism with one another and execute identical programs. An error in one processing unit is manifested as a disagreement that is visible to the other two processing units in the triad. These two units continue to the end of the current job step, at which time all essential data will have been sent to memory. Before these two processing units embark on another job step, the unit in disagreement will be taken off line and replaced with a spare. Several triads are envisioned to be multiprocessing, i.e. working independently of one another and simultaneously on different job steps such as for multi-loop control applications. Single processors are typically multiprogrammed to resemble a group of smaller processors in order to handle such applications.

Memory triads

Similarly memory modules are assigned to groups of three, called memory triads. The three members of a memory triad operate in bit synchronism with one another and store identical data. A single error in one memory unit is manifested as a disagreement visible to all three processing units of the processor triad that is communicating with the given memory triad at the time the disagreement occurs. An error committed when data are being stored does not produce a disagreement until the data are subsequently fetched. It will be necessary for error detection purposes to ensure that all data of consequence are read at least once during every test cycle of the system. The test cycle is a period during which every hardware element needed for error detection and recovery is exercised to prove its capability. At the earliest opportunity following the detection of a memory unit error, the failing memory unit will be retired and replaced by a spare. The spare will be assigned to the same address space as the two modules it is joining. The new memory unit must then be initiated by bringing its content into agreement with its partners. This is done with software, and can either be carried out immediately or on a more leisurely schedule.

Bus triad

The third class of reconfigurable unit is the bus (Fig. 7.4b). Two different redundant sets of buses are used in this system. The first is the set that communicates between processor triads and memory triads. It is a high speed serial channel which is time-shared among all active units. The second

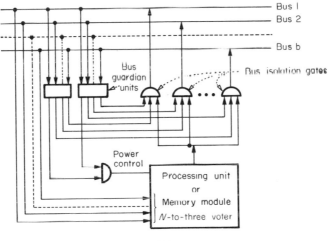

(b)

Fig. 7.4b FTMP bus system.

bus set communicates between external data sources and destinations, and a single processor triad designated as the triad responsible for input and output. The second bus set constitutes a slower serial channel which is accessible by all processing units, but used only by those which are members of the input–output processor triad. For the sake of brevity, the second bus is not considered in detail. Hereafter the term bus refers to a member of the processor–memory bus set, unless otherwise specified.

Unlike processing units and memories, bus triads do not operate independently of one another. Only one bus triad is operational until a failure necessitates a change. Three buses operate in bit synchronism carrying messages between processor triads. One processor triad at a time controls the bus, with control being granted on a demand basis. All other buses, if any, are spares. In those cases where more than one processor requests use of the bus, bus access is granted to the processor with highest priority. Priority is a concatenation of two numbers. The high-order number is the priority level of the process currently being executed by the processor. The low-order number is processor or triad priority, equal to the triad's identification number. Process priority always prevails over processor priority. Processor priority is used only to arbitrate between competitive triad requests of equal process priority. This gives a slight bias on execution speed in favour of the highest ranking processor triads. This bias may be used or ignored.

When a bus fails, the initial symptoms are like those of processing unit or memory unit failures. However, detailed examination of the error information being entered into the diagnostic data base will localize the source of error. A diagnostic program is responsible for interpreting the diagnostic data base whenever abnormal symptoms have been recorded. As soon as possible, the offending bus will be retired in favour of one of the spares. For intermitten errors, a software strategy will seek out the true cause over a period of time.

7.3   Software Redundancy

The hardest problem in achieving highly reliable computers is the validation of software. There are no guidelines for measuring or testing software reliability that are comparable to hardware reliability. The reliability of fault-tolerant computers usually assume fault-free software. The replication of software does not resolve the problem of reliability since the mistakes are also replicated.

Software redundancy is mainly used to supplement hardware redundancy. Thus when a hardware fault occurs, it is the software's job to initiate the appropriate recovery action. The degree of software–hardware mix for dealing with fault-tolerance changes according to the design style adopted. In addition to fault handling, software also permits preventive actions to be taken by special diagnostic programs which exercise the hardware systematically to ensure the absence of faults.

Here we present several approaches developed for completely different application environments.

Tandem Approach

The first system to be considered is the Tandem machine which is designed to provide a cost-effective, reliable computer for processing commercial transactions [9]. Although the Tandem machine is not based on microprocessors, many of the ideas developed are clearly applicable to multi-microprocesor systems used for similar applications. The following goals were the objectives of the Tandem computer design.

1. Non-stop computing: This implies that' when failures are detected, components are automatically taken out of service, and that repaired components can be reintegrated without stopping the system.
2. Data integrity: A continuously available system is useless if the data stored in it cannot be retrieved undamaged. Single failures of hardware modules must not damage stored data or make it inaccessible.
3. Modular expansion: As more processing power and peripheral storage capacity are needed, modules can be added to the system without any changes to application software.
4. Standard software: The programming languages provided by Tandem (COBOL, FORTRAN, and TAL, a systems programming language), are compatible with industrial standards; and all software tools necessary to develop an application are available.
5. High transactions per second per cost: This requires reasonable compromises between state-of-the-art technology, and components and methods which are known to be reliable.

The Tandem hardware organization is a multicomputer system (Fig. 7.5). Each system has between 2 and 16 computers (processor modules) in it. There is no sharing of main memory. Each processor module consists of a CPU, main memory, and an input–output channel. There is also an interface to the "Dynabus", an interprocessor communication medium that is completely independent of the input–output channels. The Dynabus consists of two independent buses, each capable of 13·3 Mbytes/s instantaneous transmission rate.

Each input–output channel is of the block multiplexer type, with block reconnect size independently set for each input–output controller. Every input–output controller connects to two input–output channels, and therefore to two processor modules. At any one time, an input–output channel may have up to 256 concurrent DMA transfers under way.

Each processor module can be receiving simultaneously on each of the two buses, with very little interference to the CPU instruction flow until the end of message input. Each processor module is powered independently. Each input–output controller is powered from two sides.

Other features which assist in maintaining the integrity of the system are as follows.

1. Duplicate (mirror) disc volumes can be maintained for each logical volume.

2. Main memory, when it is semiconductor, has single-error-correction capability.
3. There is a port for remote diagnosis.

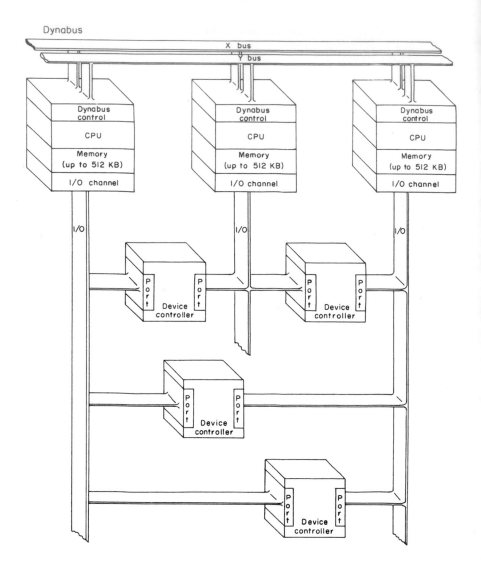

Fig. 7.5 Organization of Tandem computer (courtesy Tandem Corporation).

Overview of operating system structure

Before describing the details of process structure and programming, an overview of the operating system will be summarized.

The operating system is duplicated in every processor module. The elementary software module is the process. All interprocess communication is via a message system. This achieves geographical independence of processes and their intercommunication.

Input–output is performed by sending messages to the system-provided input–output processes. This achieves geographical independence of input–output. All system provided input–output processes are paired.

Some file system routines (procedures) run in the user (application) process's environment.

For reliable operation, processes may be paired. An identical backup copy of the process is in a second processor module, but it lies inactive until a failure occurs. State information is sent to the backup copy at user-defined checkpoints.

In case of a processor module or input–output channel or bus failure during input–output the operating system will automatically initiate input–output re-try via an alternative hardware path.

A process is created by specifying a program file, a processor module number, and (optionally) a process path.

Processes in each processor module are multiprogrammed; scheduling is pre-emptive and by priority, with run-to-completion (there is no time-slicing).

System generated messages are sent to user processes, if desired, to advise of processor module failure and other significant events, such as process termination.

There is no assembly language. All system programs are written in TAL, an Algol-like high level language.

Memory management is demand paged virtual memory.

A processor module, a peripheral controller, or a bus may be removed from operation manually or automatically (upon detection of error). Each may be reintegrated manually without stopping the rest of the system.

Process structure

Figure 7.6 shows the typical structure of a transaction-processing application in a Tandem system. A terminal screen is formatted by a user-written screen driver process, which uses the system-provided terminal input–output process to access the terminal. After input, the screen driver sends a message to another user-written process, the transaction server processor. It does data-base operations using the system-provided disc input–output

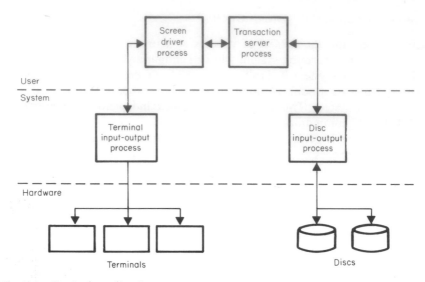

Fig. 7.6   Typical application program structure.

process(es). Information to be displayed on the terminal screen is returned to the screen driver in a message. The processes shown here may be in the same or in different processor modules.

Figure 7.7 shows that a typical application process consists of a number of procedures, including a main procedure. To implement input–output and interprocess communication, these procedures call on various system procedures.

Figure 7.8 shows more details of the program environment in a process. We are concentrating now on one process in a single processor module.

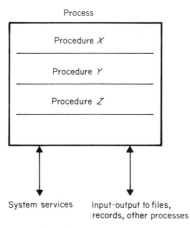

Fig. 7.7   Structure of an application process.

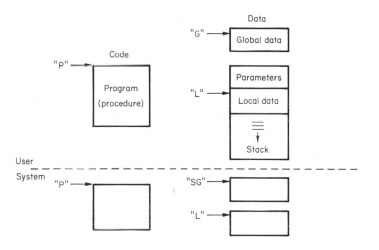

Fig. 7.8   Process programming environment.

There are four segments, or logical address spaces. The user code segment is read-only, and contains the program instructions and constants. The user data segment has all variables and data buffers. These are addressable as global variables, in the lower portion of the logical address space, or as part of the stack, which includes procedure parameters, local data, and dynamically allocated variables. These two segments are the only ones that can be addressed using a user-written procedure.

Two other segments are accessible to the operating system procedures. The system code contains the operating system procedure instructions and constants. For example, when a user procedure executes a CALL READ (file number, . . .) line, a file system procedure is invoked in the system code area. System data has the system tables, input–output buffers, and control blocks. The dynamic stack space for system procedures called by user code is in the user data segment.

For input–output operations, a user process calls on a system procedure (see the block marked "input–output system" in Fig. 7.9). After determining which input–output process will implement the input–output, the system procedure (running in the user process environment) sends a message to the appropriate input–output process (shown as *disc process*, in Fig. 7.9). *Disc process* does the input operation and then returns the data in a message.

Now let us consider the multiple computer environment. Figure 7.10 shows how inter-process communication occurs. Inter-process input–output is similar to the file example given above. Process A does an OPEN operation of process B by name. This causes process B to receive a system-

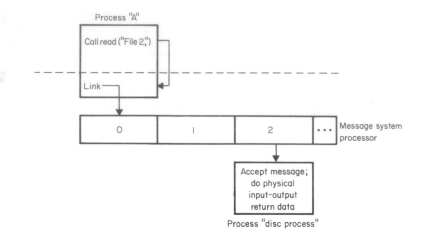

Fig. 7.9   Input-output request handling.

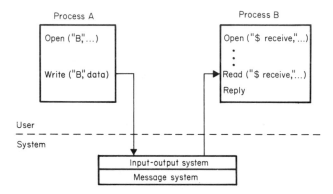

Fig. 7.10   Inter-process input-output.

generated "OPEN" message in its "RECEIVE" file input queue. There-after, as process A does WRITEs to B, process B can read them by perform-ing READs of file RECEIVE. An optional call to REPLY by process B allows the status information to be returned to process A for a given WRITE operation.

Paired processes

Figure 7.11 shows a pair of processes with the same name. To allow instant recovery (within seconds), processes can be paired. If a hardware or software failure causes the "primary" copy of the process to stop, its "backup" copy takes over.

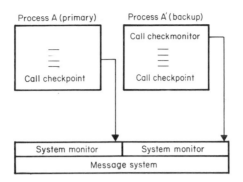

Fig. 7.11   A paired process.

The backup copy is always located in a different hardware processor module from the primary copy. It is normally an exact bit-for-bit copy of the primary process. During normal operation, only the primary copy is kept running; the backup copy awaits activation. Since each processor module is multiprogrammed, every processor in the system is able to do useful work at all times.

Periodically, the primary process will call the CHECKPOINT system procedure. This causes current state information to be moved over to the backup copy in the other processor module. A system procedure in the backup copy sets the state of the backup copy to be the same as that of the primary copy. The backup copy remains dormant.

If a failure occurs before the next CHECKPOINT call or before exit from the main procedure, the backup is activated by returning to the last CHECKPOINT call line, just as if the backup copy had made the call.

Let us now see, step by step, how the paired processes are created and activated.

Process A is created (by some ancestor process or by the operating system) and begins to run. Process A asks the operating system whether A is a backup process. If it is not, A asks whether a backup process exists. If one does not, A calls a system procedure to create A', a backup copy of process A. The backup copy, A', is created in another processor module. Process A' asks the operating system whether A' is a backup process. It is, so it goes to sleep by calling CHECKMONITOR. Process A opens the files it will use by calling OPEN. It then opens them again on behalf of its backup copy by calling CHECKOPEN. Process A begins processing. At points decided on by the application programmer, A calls CHECKPOINT. This causes the current stack state and the current file status to be sent from A to its backup copy A', in the other processor module. The state information is stored into the virtual memory of the sleeping backup copy, and the file status is stored into its file control blocks.

Process A continues processing. Let us assume that there is a failure in the processor in which A is executing, or that the process stops for some other reason, after some more processing has occurred, possibly including a disc WRITE call.

The system monitor in the processor module where A' resides detects the failure, either by receiving a message from the other system monitor, or by noticing that no "I'm alive" messages have been received recently from the primary process' CPU. It activates A' by doing a return to the last CHECKPOINT call line. (Remember that the stack state of A' was set up at the time of the last CHECKPOINT call by A'.)

A' continues processing. It attempts the input–output operations possibly already done by A since the last CHECKPOINT call. However, the system input–output processes keep synchronization information for every input–output operation. The completion status of all successfully completed input–output operations is returned to A', without trying the operations again.

Later in its processing loop, A' may ask the operating system whether a backup copy exists. Since one does not exist, it may create a new backup copy, or it may wait until a failed processor has been repaired and reintegrated before recreating a copy of itself. In either case, it may also voluntarily switch primary/backup roles with its copy, by calling CHECKSWITCH.

PLURIBUS

One early architecture using a minicomputer for fault-tolerant operations is the Pluribus structure [11] (Fig. 7.12).

The Pluribus system consists of a set of modules which fall into three types. The first type contains one or more computers (Lockheed SUE processors plus local memory); the second, collections of memory modules (to serve as shared memory); and the third, input–output and clock devices. All these modules are connected by a redundant point-to-point communica-

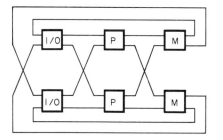

Fig. 7.12 The PLURIBUS structure.

tion system. For example, a small system might consist of two computer modules having independent connections to two memory modules, and two input–output modules, each connected to the two memory modules.

Pluribus uses software to provide most of its fault tolerance. Data structures are constructed redundantly so that they can be checked for correctness. Time-out counters are employed for hardware/software fault detection, and many system functions require concurrence of several processors before they are executed.

The Pluribus serves as an IMP (interface message processor) in the Arpanet. Its goal is high availability. An occasional dropped message or brief stoppage is acceptable, but the system must recover within a few seconds so as not to disrupt network users. Pluribus is operational and has exceeded its requirements with an availability of $99 \cdot 9\%$.

SIFT

The SIFT (software implemented fault-tolerance) system, designed at Stanford Research Institute International, is an ultra-reliable computer that achieves fault-tolerance by replicating tasks among processing units [12]. Error detection and fault isolation are achieved by software.

Fault-tolerant computer systems vary greatly in their reliability requirements. A typical requirement in space applications is for a probability of between 95 and 99% that computing capability will exist after 5 to 10 years of operation. This implies a mean time between failure (MTBF) from 100 to 1000 years.* In the control of an aircraft, at which this design was aimed, the requirement was for a probability of failure less than 10^{-8} during a 10-hour operational period. This translates to an MTBF of 10^4 years, i.e. 10 to 100 times more stringent than the above. The consequences of failure (the possible loss of human lives and economic loss) is, in this application, extremely high and justifies the use of extensive redundancy in the computer system where cost is, even with redundancy, a small proportion of total aircraft cost. The computing load for this application is such that the computer must have approximately 16 k words of memory and be capable of more than $0 \cdot 5$ MIPS.† Assuming LSI circuitry with a chip-failure probability of 10^{-6} per hour, the overall system design must allow for correct functional behaviour in the presence of multiple chip failures, which can be expected in a computer system containing several hundred LSI chips.

*This statement does not imply that a single computer will survive for 100 to 1000 years, but that n such computers will, after y years, have suffered $n.y/100$ or $n.y/1000$ failures.

†Millions of instructions per second.

Faults in the two major subsystems, i.e. the processor and the memory are considered. With reasonable predictions of LSI development over the next few years, analysis shows that the processor will need approximately 10% of the chips required for the memory. Therefore, replication of the processor could be regarded as an economic checking and fault-masking technique. Protection of the memory function can be carried out either by replication or coding or by a combination of both. The system described here uses memory replication, but the basic concepts are compatible with alternative methods for protecting the memory.

The system described has many properties that, in total, distinguish it from other fault-tolerant systems.

1. Replicated units do not operate in lock-step mode, but are only loosely synchronized. The communication between CPUs is asynchronous thereby removing the need for an ultrareliable system clock.
2. Agreement between replicated units is verified only at the completion of program segments (tasks).
3. Faulty units are not necessarily removed but can either be ignored or assigned to tasks having no overall effect.
4. Transient faults do not necessarily cause permanent removal of the faulty units. Furthermore the looseness of synchronization among sets of tasks makes it possible to enhance immunity from transient faults, by ensuring that redundant versions of a computation may be done at times.
5. The degree of fault tolerance can be different for different tasks being performed, and can be different at different times for the same task.
6. No special hardware is used to carry out fault detection or correction.
7. Communication between CPUs is minimized so that low bandwidth buses can be used, thereby facilitating the physical separation of modules in environments where physical damage is a hazard.
8. The design concept is independent of the way in which the units are built, i.e. no specialization of CPU or memory design is required for fault tolerance, thereby allowing the choice to be based on other properties, e.g. speed, availability.
9. The total computing power of the system can be varied by using units of different speed or by changing the number of units.

The system (Fig. 7.13) consists of a number of modules, each composed of a memory and a processing unit. The individual processing units within the modules are connected to the corresponding memory units with wide bandwidth buses. The intermodule bus organization (B_1, B_2, B_3) is designed to allow a processor to read from any memory but not to write into other memory units. The intermodule bus is expected to have a much lower bandwidth than an intramodule bus. The bus logic envisioned does not use

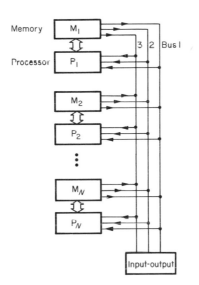

Memory

M_1

3 2 Bus I

Processor P_1

M_2

P_2

$\vdots$

M_N

P_N

Input-output

Fig. 7.13   SIFT system configuration.

voting. The number there is chosen for convenience of discussion.

The input–output system, discussed in a later section, is assumed to be connected to buses B_1, B_2, and B_3. The input–output system shown in Fig. 7.13 consists of all the non-computing units, such as transducers, actuators, and sensors. The part of the total input–output that is carried out by the program, like formatting or code conversion, is handled in the same manner as any other task, and is replicated in several processors.

The system is viewed as being regular in that no module is *a priori* assigned a special role. All computations that require high reliability are carried out in several modules. We assume for the purpose of this description that critical tasks are processed in three units.

The computations that must be carried out are broken into a number of tasks in such a way that no task requires more computing power than can be supplied by one processor. The tasks are given the designations, A, B, C, ...; the processors are numbered 1, 2, 3, ... Each processor is capable of being multiprogrammed over a number of tasks, as illustrated in Fig. 7.14.

Control of the computing system is carried out by an executive system that can be segmented by function into two parts:

1. local executive: functions that apply to each processor (e.g. dispatching,* reporting errors, loading new task programs);

---

*Dispatching is the executive function that initiates a new task at the completion of the previous one.

Processors

	1	2	3	4	5	6	...	n
A	X	X		X				
B		X		X	X			
C		X						
D	X		X	X				
E		X		X	X			
F			X		X	X		
G	X	X	X					
H	X			X		X		
I	X		X		X			
J	X	X	X	X	X	X		
⋮								
N								

Tasks

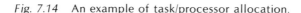

Fig. 7.14   An example of task/processor allocation.

2. system executive: functions that are global to the system (e.g. the allocation and scheduling of work load, reconfiguring).

A complete set of the software functions of class 1 is present in each processor; those in class 2 are carried out in a sufficient number of processors to provide the degree of fault-tolerance required. The functions are realized by programs that have the same task structure as all other programs.

The normal operating mode for a processor carrying out a task is to follow the flow of control shown in Fig. 7.15. Data required for the task are assumed to have been computed by several processors (including possibly the same one carrying out the task). A check is made to see if the data are available in all processors. If not, the fact is noted in the memory of the module and the dispatcher program within the module is entered to determine the next task to be processed. The next processing is the reading

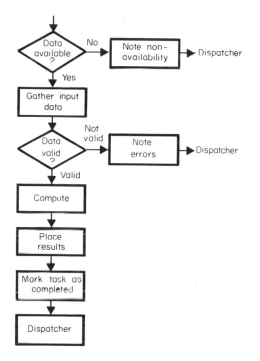

Fig. 7.15   Typical task flow.

of input data from the several processors where copies exist. A validation is now carried out, typically by a two-out-of-three vote. If any of the copies of the input data are found not to agree, then this is noted for later processing by the executive. If all the copies are different, this is noted and control moves to the dispatcher program. Otherwise the computation of the task is now carried out, the results are left in the memory of the module, and note is made (in the module) of the fact that the task is computed.

The following important principles apply in the above scheme.

1. No processor writes into the memory of another module.
2. Input data in a module are not destroyed during the computation: if the computation is repetitive, the results of one cycle that may be used as input for the next cycle are placed in a different location in memory. Similarly, because the input data within one module may be needed later by another processor carrying out the same task, the input data must not be destroyed until all co-operating processors have read, validated, and used the data. This may mean that the data are preserved over several iterations if they are used by another task that is delayed behind the first.

3. All conditions (e.g. errors, task complete) are left as notes to be read later by the system executive.
4. The dispatcher program, which exists in each module, maintains a queue of tasks to be computed. The data for this queue are read from the memories of the modules that are running the executive. The flow of control of the dispatcher is itself similar to that shown in Fig. 7.15, except at the end, when control is transferred to the task that is at the head of the queue.
5. The dispatcher in each processor checks periodically to see if the system executive has changed the queue of tasks for that processor. A single bit (per processor) is set in the system executive tables to indicate a change of the queue. If this bit is not set, the dispatcher waits some time (e.g. 1 ms) before querying it again, thereby preventing continuous interrogation and consequent heavy intermodule bus traffic.

The above scheme has a degree of fault tolerance with no special hardware requirements on the memory or processor units. In particular, an erroneous calculation carried out by a module does not destroy the validity of the total system, because results are rejected by the next calculation.

An important benefit in using software techniques for fault detection and tolerance is that freedom is retained to change the degree of fault tolerance, either because experience provides data on which better methods can be based, or because the different applications require different degrees of fault tolerance, i.e. some are more critical than others.

If threefold replication is used throughout the system, a single faulty unit will cause one of the replicated processes to compute a wrong result. The use of the wrong result in subsequent calculations will be avoided since other (correct) copies of the data will exist in other modules and when used will, by voting, enable a processor to distinguish the correct data from that which is erroneous.

Consider now the case of double faults existing simultaneously. We must distinguish two cases, uncorrelated and correlated faults. By correlated faults we mean two faults that cause the computation of two equal but incorrect results. Clearly, two correlated faults cannot be tolerated if the fault-tolerance procedure consists merely of voting among three versions of all results. The probability of such correlated faults will be extremely low and for most applications is acceptable. However, in the system described, greater reliability can be achieved in the event that the application is so critical that this low probability is still unacceptable. Two strategies are:

1. use threefold replication for all critical applications, and, in the event of any disagreement, do not use the results until yet further processors have carried out a repetition of the calculation, for example use two

more processors (making a total of five) and only act if three or more
agree;
2. use fivefold (or greater) replication of tasks for all critical applications.
This requires availability of a sufficient number of the various units
(processors, memories, buses).

Both of the above strategies will prevent double correlated errors from
causing a wrong result to be used in subsequent programs or output. The
cost penalty in the above strategies is such that they should only be used for
extremely critical applications, where the cost of extra computing
equipment is small compared with the penalty for failure, e.g. in aircraft
and space missions.

In the case of double uncorrelated faults, we need only consider the case
of simultaneous faults. Double faults that occur which are separated
sufficiently in time for the executive to have carried out corrective action
after the first fault do not need to be regarded as different from two
instances of single faults, which can be tolerated.

Two simultaneous but uncorrelated faults will have the possible effect of
producing two different incorrect results from a calculation. These two
results will be compared with the one correct result produced by the non-
faulty unit in a threefold replication scheme. Before the result is used in any
subsequent calculation (or output), the presence of three different results
will be detected and the executive will initiate greater replication in other
processors until there is sufficient agreement to distinguish the correct from
the incorrect result.

In considering the effect of multiple faults in the system, an improvement
in reliability is achieved because multiple processors are not operating in a
lock-step mode. A short term, widespread transient in the system hardware
(e.g. power supply or bus system) will not necessarily cause errors in the
same application programs in the processors, thereby increasing the
probability of being able to detect and correct the errors from the transient.

The executive of the system must itself be fault-tolerant. This is achieved
by the same techniques as for application programs. Each of the replicated
copies of the executive will use data from itself and the other copies. In
the event of errors in one of the executives, the other copies will not use the
data computed by it, thereby keeping their results valid. The correctly
functioning copies will initiate a new copy of the executive in another
processor (which will entail copying the program to that processor) and will
signal the malfunctioning processor to discontinue processing the executive.
In addition, on inspection of the data in the correct copies of the executive
all processors will cease referencing the data in the incorrect copy, thereby
preventing a system breakdown if the malfunctioning processor continues
processing the executive even though requested to discontinue.

It is expected that, in the event of a permanent fault being detected, a unit will be relieved of any active part in subsequent calculations, and the capacity of the system therefore will be reduced. However, until a large fraction of the system is faulty, the fault-tolerance procedures can be continued.

7.4   Reconfigurable Multi-microprocessor Systems

For on-line real-time applications such as control of the telephone network, a distributed multi-microprocessor network is applicable [13]. In such systems the various nodes that constitute the microcomputers are interconnected by means of communication lines. The overall structure is of interest from the point of view of fault tolerance, to ensure that a line or node failure does not cripple the system. The total network could also have sufficient computational power so that the failure of a node would result in re-distribution of the computing load. The communication system clearly needs to have redundancy so that the failure of a link does not make some parts of the network inaccessible to others. The failure of a node may not be tolerated in certain applications if the node is used to control critical equipment. In those situations a fault-tolerant design needs to be applied when building the node computer.

In such loosely coupled distributed multi-microprocessor systems it is worthwhile considering the problem of reconfigurability. This means that the topological changes due to failures or bringing in spare parts are recognized by the rest of the system and the overall network survives such faults or adapts itself to new situations by reconfiguring itself. VTM offers just such an architecture, as explained below.

VTM System

One of the major objectives of the VTM systems is to be able to rearrange the configurations to match the needs of different applications. A flexible system should include provisions for insertions (extensions) and deletions (reductions).

In general, a node in a system becomes aware of the entire configuration either by a network control centre (NCC) or as a result of distributed exchange of the configuration (topology) information. The NCC approach can be utilized to implement a fixed routing mechanism. The necessary routing tables, which are computed using the system topology information, are distributed to the participating nodes, once and for all. For a VTM system which does not have an NCC, it is necessary to compute routing tables externally and to provide each node with a copy of the full configuration information. Given the network topology, the shortest distance algorithms, such as Dijkstra's algorithm, can be used to compute all the shortest paths between the local node and the rest of the system [14].

The provision of a distributed reconfiguration mechanism eliminates the need for a network control centre and a copy of the full configuration information at each node. Instead, each node is responsible for maintaining partial routing information so as to be able to communicate to its neighbouring nodes.

The handling of configurational changes in multi-computer systems is a necessary part of their design. It is required for reliability, modularity, and extensibility. It is the dynamical reconfiguration which is important. The routing mechanisms, such as

random,
flooding,
ideal observer, and
adaptive,

can respond dynamically to the changes. The first two techniques can utilize any live link and node. A node is not necessarily aware of the full system topology. The third technique needs a network control centre which ideally is assumed to watch the entire system and is responsible for incorporating traffic and topology changes. The last technique, i.e. adaptive routing, is basically a flow control mechanism which can also respond to the topology changes in terms of some delay function.

In this section, a communication mechanism based on the exchange of the distributed topology information is discussed. A particular reconfiguration technique is proposed to handle the exchange of topology information and thus to maintain the necessary routing tables. A topology message is sent only if there is an indication of a change in the configuration. This mechanism handles the reconfiguration dynamically. The link, node, or link and node failures and the reverse changes, i.e. new link, new node, or new link and node cases, are made known to every live node in the system in a finite time.

The proposed reconfiguration technique is discussed in connection with uniform and dense networks. It is based on Baran's hot-potato routine [15]. A correctness proof of a similar algorithm has also been presented by Tajibnapis [16].

The proposed reconfiguration algorithm is basically an adaptive algorithm. It is intended, however, to be controlled by the configurational changes rather than traffic changes. It will initialize the system by setting the initial configuration and then adapt the system, dynamically, to further possible changes in topology. The changes occur either as a result of failures (link, node link, and node) or as a result of new links, nodes, or links and nodes joining the system. The topology message format is as shown as follows:

HEADER	DESTINATION	SOURCE	DISTANCE	CRC

Initialization

Given a network of N nodes, it first undergoes an initialization phase whereby each node detects the adjacent operable links and thus exchanges this information with neighbouring nodes. The information is passed in the form of standard format units (topology messages). The new neighbour receives the full account of the topology information available at the detecting node, in the form of one topology message per accessible node. Note that the links are assumed to be bi-directional, i.e. if a link (a, b) is live so is the link (b, a). In practice this is not always the case.

The topology message contains two fields relevant to reconfiguration: identification of destination node i and the shortest distance between the sending node s and node i. A node generates, and may modify, a shortest distance table as shown in Fig. 7.16. The entries are indexed by the node identification and the entries themselves are the shortest distance between the corresponding destination node and the local node.

Destination	Distance
0	d(0)
1	d(1)
2	d(2)
.	.
.	.
.	.
k	d(k)
.	.
.	.
.	.
$n-1$	d($n-1$)

Fig. 7.16   Shortest distance table at node K.

Handling insertion of a new node

Now, suppose that node 1 of Fig. 7.17 detects a new neighbour, say node 17 in the same figure, and the rest of the system is uniform with the configuration known and node 17 has no ties with any other node in the system, except node 1. This is a major change in the network. The topology message exchange propagates until the configurational change has been detected at every node in the system. A receiving node needs to send topology messages to its neighbouring nodes only if the topology message received has changed the previous topology information, i.e. the shortest distance table.

This process can best be visualized by a top-down tree, as shown in Fig. 7.18. The tree is extracted from the network shown in Fig. 7.17. The

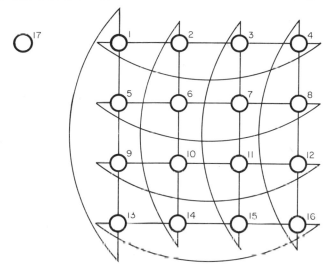

Fig. 7.17 Node insertion.

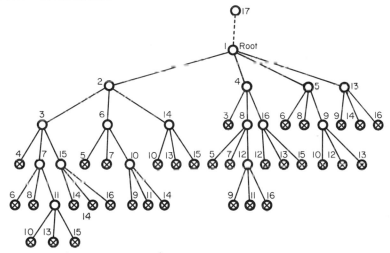

Fig. 7.18 Topology message exchange tree.

messages on the topological changes originated at node 1 stop at the terminal nodes when the configuration information, i.e. the shortest distance table, has reached settlement. Note that the branches represent the communication links and the vertices represent the nodes as numbered in Fig. 7.18. A node is crossed if it has already been traversed once by an equivalent topology message. Two topology messages are considered equivalent if the destination field, the distance field, and the sending node are the same. For this example a node is traversed at least once for the configurational change to be transparent to the system since node 17 has no ties with the rest of the network. However, the node may have to be traversed more than once in cases where the network is loaded with other traffic which may cause delays on certain paths. The topology messages that then take longer paths can reach a node before those taking shorter paths. The distance and the routing tables alter every time a topology change on a shorter path arrives. Every change is then fanned through the system.

Starting from the ROOT node 1, there are five levels of transmission. The system, with the exception of node 17, is expected to settle in five main periods. For node 17, however, $(n-1)$ main periods are required to receive the complete topology information from the ROOT, where n is the number of nodes in the original network. This is because the ROOT needs to send the shortest path vector to node 17, where each path is transmitted in the form of a topology change message.

In practice, a new link does not always belong to a first-time node joining the system. The node might already have been taking part in the system. On the other hand, more than one link can become live at the same time. This occurs if one or more nodes join the system all at once, with all the adjacent links coming up simultaneously.

Handling failed links

Link failures are handled differently. Obviously a failed link cannot take part in a transmission. Upon detection of a failed link out of $m + 1$ links, the prepared topology message only needs to be broadcast over the remaining m links. From then on, the procedure for handling a topology message is the same as for the live link detection case. Now, for clarity suppose that the failure of a particular link disconnects the adjacent node from the rest of the system, which is the reverse of the node insertion case discussed in the previous example. The failure of the link (1, 17) causes the system in Fig. 7.17 to settle in five main periods. This is because the system requires five levels of transmission (see Fig. 7.18).

Implementing the reconfiguration algorithm

A network of needs to be reconfigured if one of the following topological changes occurs:

1. a new link is introduced (or a failed link is repaired and returned to the system);
2. a new node is joined to the system (or a failed node is repaired and re-inserted);

3. a link fails;
4. a node fails.

It is important that a topological change of a permanent nature is made known to the entire network in a finite time. This is where the reconfiguration mechanism comes in. It controls the flow of topological information both distributedly and dynamically. On the other hand, temporary changes such as short time link, node, or link and node failures need not be fanned through the system. Instead a temporary blockage on the failed unit, or re-routing at the adjacent nodes, can be more advantageous until the failure state is removed. This is because the global reconfiguration mechanisms use up an important fraction of the available communication capacity of the network which would otherwise be utilized for the actual information transmission. For permanent failures, however, the reconfiguration mechanism pays off with higher reliability, adaptability, and extensibility.

In a real life system, permanent and temporary configuration changes need to be distinguished before taking any action. This can be handled by employing a re-try and time-out mechanism. Before declaring a failure as permanent the detecting node waits for a finite duration of time during which the failure is declared temporary and the necessary precautions are taken accordingly. This mechanism can also be used for the new links or nodes joining the system. However, a live link or a live node detection mechanism can be incorporated with the type of joining, i.e. whether it is a permanent attachment or a temporary one. Reconfiguration is considered only for the practical case of permanent topological changes.

Data base of the reconfiguration algorithm

The reconfiguration algorithm operates basically on two tables. The distance table (DT) which records the distance (path length) of each node in the system from the host node via each of the neighbouring nodes; the routing table (RT) which records the shortest paths only. For each destination a maximum of m paths can be identified, where m is the number of neighbours. The DT is an n by m table, where n is the network size. Figure 7.19 shows the DT a node 1 of the 16-node network given in Fig. 7.17. In a regularly connected homogenous network all the distance tables are of equal size. An entry $d(k,i,j)$ is the distance of path (k,i) via the neighbour $X(j)$, where $i = 1,2 \ldots , n$ and $j = 1,2, \ldots , m$. The nodes that are not accessible from node k have a corresponding entry of infinity in the table. For example, node 1 appears inaccessible from itself via any of its neighbours.

The size of the routing table (RT) depends upon the specific routing mechanism being employed. In fact, RT is arranged using the distance

Destination	Via neighbouring nodes			
	2	4	5	13
1	∞	∞	∞	∞
2	1	3	3	3
3	2	2	4	4
.				
.				
.				
16	4	2	4	2

Fig. 7.19   Distance table for node 1 of a 16-node network.

table. An entry $r(i,k)$ or RT indicates the neighbour node, say $X(j)$, via which the node i is at a minimum distance from the host node k, i.e.

$$d_m(k,i,j) = \min_{l \leq m} (d(k,i,l)).$$

The entries of RT change only if the minimum of the corresponding DT row changes. It would save processing time if a shortest distance (SD) table were used alongside the distance table. We have

$$SD(i) = d_m(k,i,j).$$

Figure 7.20 gives the routing table and the shortest distance table related to the distance table given in Fig. 7.19. Note that $r(l,l) = 0$ and SD(1) is infinity which means that node 1 cannot send a message to itself by means of routing tables. For applications where the communication protocols maintain information flow between the processes rather than the processors (nodes) independent of where they are residing, we can have SD(k) non-infinity, where $r(k,k) = 0$.

The reconfiguration algorithm operates on those entries which are related to the topological changes. For example, if a topological change concerns node 1, only the ith level of distance, routing, and shortest distance tables need to be referred to after detection. An exception is the detection of the change which requires either the shortest distance table to be sent to the new neighbour or the column of the distance table corresponding to the failed link to be updated.

Destination	Next node		Shortest distance
1	0		∞
2	2		1
3	2		2
.	.		.
.	.		.
.	.		.
15	4		3
16	13		2
(a)			(b)

Fig. 7.20   Routing tables at node 1 of a 16-node network. (a) Routing table (RT).
(b) Shortest distance table (SD).

The reconfiguration algorithm

The reconfiguration algorithm is structured into three basic subalgorithms. Algorithm 1 handles the link and/or node failures. A node failure is interpreted as the simultaneous failure of the links. Algorithm 2 handles a new link and/or node coming up. A node is declared new if all the links connected to it become alive simultaneously. Algorithm 3 handles the

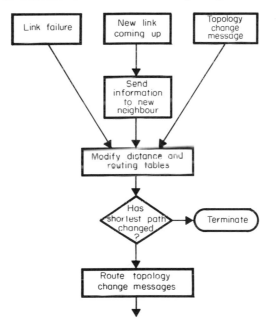

Fig. 7.21   Organization of reconfiguration algorithm.

topology messages which indicate the configurational changes. These algorithms are given in detail in Table 7.I. A reconfiguration protocol is complete only with a specific routing mechanism, queue management algorithms, and input–output handling routines at the lower level of communication. Figure 7.21 shows a system flow diagram of the reconfiguration mechanism excluding the flow level communication protocol routines. A more detailed description of three algorithms has been written by Bozyigit [14]. Some simulation results using the reconfiguration algorithm are reported by Bozyigit and Paker [17].

Table 7.I   Reconfiguration algorithms.

Nomenclature for the reconfiguration algorithms

a = source node
n = destination node
c = node adjacent (neighbour) to node a
$d_{b,j}^{a}$ = distance between a and b via the jth neighbour of a (the superscript a is omitted wherever it is obvious)
r_{b}^{a} = the first neighbour on shortest path between a and b indicated by a neighbour of a on that path

TM_{b}^{a} = topology message compiled at a to be sent to b
$c \leftarrow TM_{b}^{a}$ = send TM_{b}^{a} to c
V_{b}^{a} = shortest distance between a and b
W_{c}^{a} = weight of link between a and c
X_{i}^{a} = ith neighbour of a
t = a temporary variable

Algorithm 1: Handles a new link coming up at node a

1. (a new link detected at the local node a)
   link (a, c) becomes live;
2. (update distance and routing tables)
   $d_{c,j}^{a} := 1$ where jth neighbour = c,
   $V_{c}^{a} := 1$,
   $r_{c}^{a} := c$;
3. (prepare topology message)
   (set distance field of topology message)
   dist $(TM_{c}^{a}) := 1$,
   (set destination field of topology message)
   dest $(TM_{c}^{a}) := c$;

4. (send topology message to neighbouring nodes)
   $X_{j}^{a} \leftarrow TM_{c}^{a}$ for $j = 1,2 \ldots, m$ and $X_{j}^{a} \neq c$;
5. (send available topology information to new neighbour)
   (form topology message)
   dist $(TM_{j}^{a}) := V_{j}^{a}$,
   dest $(TM_{j}^{a}) := i$ for $i = 1,2, \ldots, n$.
   (send topology change messages to new neighbour)
   $TM_{j}^{c} := TM_{j}^{a}$;
6. Exit.

(cont.)

Table 7.1   *(cont.)*

Algorithm 2: Handles link failures at node a

1. (a link failure detected at node a)
   link (a, c) failed;
2. (update the distance table)
   (save distance vector corresponding
   to failed link)
   $t_j := d^a_{i,j}$,
   (set vector $d^a_{i,j}$ to infinity)
   $d^a_{i,j} := \infty$ where $X^a_j = c$, and $i =$
   $\quad$ 1,2,3, $\ldots$, n;
   $\quad j =$ index of the failed
   $\quad$ link
3. (update routing tables and prepare
   topology messages)
   for $i :=$ from 1 to n with step 1 do

if $V^a_j = t_j$ then
$\quad V^a_j := \min|d^a_{i,j}|, j \in m$
$\quad r^a_j := X^a_j$ where $V^a_j = d^a_{i,j}$,
$\quad TM^a_i := V^a_i$,
$\quad$ (send topology message).
$\quad TM^{x^{aj}}_i := IM^a_i$ for
$\quad j = 1,2, \ldots, m$, except for
$\quad X^a_i = c$,
fi,
od;
4. Exit.

Algorithm 3: Handles arrived topology message at node a

1. (detect topology message at local
   node a)
   TM^c_b arrives at a;
2. (update distance and routing tables)
   (assign new distance for (a, b) path)
   $d^a_{b,j} := IM^c_b + W^a_c$,
   (find new min distance (a, b) path)
   $t_b := \min [d^a_{b,j}], j \in m$
   (assign the shortest path)
   if t_b not $= V^a_b$ then

$\quad r^a_b := X^a_j$ where $t_b = d^a_{b,l}$
$\quad V^a_b := t_b$,
(prepare topology messages)
dist $(TM^a_b) := V^a_b$,
dest $(TM^a_b) := b^a$,
(send topology message to
neighbours)
$\quad X^a_j \leftarrow TM^a_b$ for all $j \in m$.
fi;
3. Exit.

Algorithm 4: Round-robin routing algorithm

1. (input a message at a) TM^c_b arrives
2. (find the shortest path (c, b))
   if $c = (m - 1)$ then
   $\quad c := 0$
   fi,

(next node)
$c := r^a_b$;
3. (message joins output queue)
$\quad OU_c := TM^a_b$;
4. Exit.

References

[1] R. Bernhard. The 'no-downtime' computer, *IEEE Spectrum*, September 1980, pp. 33–37.
[2] A. Avizienis. Architecture of fault tolerant computing systems, in *Digest of the 1975 International Symposium on Fault-tolerant Computing*, Paris, June 1975, pp. 3–16.
[3] J. Von Neumann. "Probabilistic Logics and the Synthesis of Reliable Organisms from Unreliable Components", Automata Structures,

C. E. Shannon and J. McCarthy, Eds, Annals of Math. Studies No. 34, Princeton University Press, 1956, pp. 93–98.

[4] D. A. Rennels. Distributed fault tolerant computer systems, *IEEE Computer*, March 1980.

[5] D. P. Siewiorek, M. Canepa and S. Clark. "C.vmp: The Analysis, Architecture, and Implementation of a Fault Tolerant Multiprocessor", Departments of Electrical Engineering and Computer Science, Carnegie-Mellon University, December 1976.

[6] A. Lunde. "Evaluation of Instruction Set Processor Architecture by Program Tracing", Communications of the ACM, February 1977.

[7] W. M. Daly, A. L. Hopkins and J. F. McKenna. A fault-tolerant digital clocking system, in *Digest of the 2nd International Symposium on fault-tolerant Computing*, Newton, Mmms. IEEE Computer Society, June 1973, pp. 17–22.

[8] A. L. Hopkins and T. B. Smith. The architectural elements of a symmetric fault tolerant multiprocessor, *IEEE Trans. on Comput.*, **C-24**, No. 5, May 1975, pp. 498–505.

[9] J. V. Levy. A multiple computer system for reliable transaction processing, *ACM SIG SMALL Newsletter*, **4**, No. 5, October 1978, pp. 5–22.

[10] Joel F. Bartless. "A 'NonStop' Operating System", *Proc. 11th Hawaii International conference on System Sciences*, January 1978, Vol. 3.

[11] B. Katsuk, *et al.* Pluribus—An operational fault-tolerant multiprocessor, *Proc. IEEE*, **66**, No. 10, October, 1978, pp. 1146–1159.

[12] J. H. Wensley. SIFT—Software implemented fault tolerance, *Fall Joint Computer Conference*, 1972.

[13] J. C. B. Missen and G. V. George. A fault tolerant multi-microprocessor: for telecommunication and general application, GEC Telecommunications Ltd. (UK).

[14] M. Bozyigit. A dense variable topology multicomputer system: specifications and performance analysis, PhD Thesis, Polytechnic of Central London, May 1979.

[15] P. Baran. On distributed communication networks, *IEEE Trans. on Communication Systems*, Vol. Comm-12, 1967, pp. 1–9.

[16] W. B. Tajibnapis. A correctness proof of a topology information maintenance protocol for a distributed computer network, *Comm. ACM*, July 1977, pp. 47–485.

[17] M. Bozyigit and Y. Paker. A topology reconfiguration mechanism for distributed computer systems, *The Computer Journal*, **25**, No. 1, 1982.

Further Reading

Bellis, H. Comparing analytical reliability models to hard and transient failure data, M.S.E.E. thesis, Department of Electrical Engineering, Carnegie-Mellon University, April 1978.

Ingle, A. and Siewiorek, D. P. Reliability modelling of multiprocessor structures, *Proc. IEEE CompCon*, September 1976.

Katzman, A. A fault-tolerant computing system, *Proc. 11th Hawaii International Conference on System Sciences*, January 1978, Vol. 3.

Parnas, D. L. Response to detected errors in well-structured programs, Carnegie-Mellon University Computer Science Department Report, 1972.

Pollack, F. J. A design methodology for fault-tolerant software, Ph.D. thesis, Carnegie-Mellon University, 1978.

Wakerly, J. F. Microcomputer reliability improvement using triple-modular redundancy, *Proceedings of the IEEE*, **64**, No. 6, June 1976, pp. 889–895.

Wensley, J. H., Levitt, K. N. and Neumann, P. G. A comparative study of architectures for fault-tolerance, in *Digest of the 4th International Symposium on Fault-tolerant Computing*, IEEE Computer Society, June, 1974.

Subject Index

A.P.I.C. Studies in Data Processing
General Editor: Fraser Duncan